TWAYNE'S WORLD AUTHORS SERIES

A Survey of the World's Literature

Sylvia E. Bowman, Indiana University

GENERAL EDITOR

FRANCE

Maxwell A. Smith, Guerry Professor of French, Emeritus
The University of Chattanooga
Visiting Professor in Modern Languages
The Florida State University

EDITOR

Joris-Karl Huysmans

(TWAS 31)

TWAYNE'S WORLD AUTHORS SERIES (TWAS)

The purpose of TWAS is to survey the major writers —novelists, dramatists, historians, poets, philosophers, and critics—of the nations of the world. Among the national literatures covered are those of Australia, Canada, China, Eastern Europe, France, Germany, Greece, India, Italy, Japan, Latin America, New Zealand, Poland, Russia, Scandinavia, Spain, and the African nations, as well as Hebrew, Yiddish, and Latin Classical literatures. This survey is complemented by Twayne's United States Authors Series and English Authors Series.

The intent of each volume in these series is to present a critical-analytical study of the works of the writer; to include biographical and historical material that may be necessary for understanding, appreciation, and critical appraisal of the writer; and to present all material in clear, concise English—but not to vitiate the scholarly content of the work by doing so.

Joris-Karl Huysmans

By GEORGE ROSS RIDGE

Louisiana State University

Twayne Publishers, Inc.   ::   New York

Preface

The very name of Joris-Karl Huysmans incarnates the decadent *fin de siècle* with more brilliance than that of any other writer of the glittering age. It never fails to evoke, somewhat nostalgically, the metaphysical spleen and the gamey diabolism of the Eighteen-Nineties, resplendent as the era was with its pornographic sketches, erotic subject matter, and involuted and sometimes scabrous prose. Even the great constellation of English Decadent writers, like Wilde, Symons, and Swinburne, acknowledge, from London, their debt of literary homage to their lodestar, the Supreme Decadent, no less than their French counterparts across the Channel in Paris. Huysmans is ever, for both groups, the archetypal Decadent. And to the present day he has retained this image in both the Gallic and Anglo-Saxon minds.

But why is this so? one wonders with cause. For Huysmans undoubtedly is a Naturalist in his early works, and evolves into a Catholic writer, and even a hagiographer, in his later works. Still, the legend of the Decadent persists. The peculiar reasons for this acclaim of Huysmans as a Decadent author, as well as for his continuing appeal to the present time, will be scrutinized in the conclusion.

A biographical sketch of Huysmans is, of course, the chronologically natural and proper subject of Chapter One. Yet, since Huysmans identifies himself so often and so closely with his various heroes, his life, or at least his intellectual and esthetic development, remains a constant source of discussion throughout the book. In this context, young Huysmans as a Naturalist is the subject of Chapter Two. Then, during his middle period, in Chapter Three, Huysmans presents himself as a "decadent," or rather as a Decadent writer. The aging Huysmans, who experiences a profound conversion after a lengthy spiritual crisis, is the subject of

Chapter Four. The conclusion, Chapter Five, summarizes the meaning and the importance of Huysmans' work in the context of the Decadent world view. Although Huysmans plays an important role in each of these aspects in the history of nineteenth century French literature, it is perhaps this last-named aspect, the significance of his Decadent philosophy to our own age, that gives him his peculiar and abiding reputation. It is in this area, too, that new work in Huysmansiana will necessarily have to be done, to help plumb the depths of one of the most complex men of his time.

GEORGE ROSS RIDGE

Tallahassee, Florida

Contents

Chronology

1848   February 5, Joris-Karl Huysmans, baptized under the name of Charles-Marie-Georges, is born in Paris, at No. 11 Rue Suger, of a Dutch father, Victor-Godfried-Jan Huysmans, and of a French mother, née Élisabeth-Malvina Badin.

1856   June 24, Godfried Huysmans dies. Autumn, young Huysmans becomes a *pensionnat* at the Institution Hortus.

1857   Malvina Huysmans marries M. Jules Og after a brief courtship.

1858   May, M. et Mme Og purchase a book bindery at No. 11 Rue de Sèvres.

1862   Joris-Karl Huysmans enrolls at the Lycée Saint-Louis.

1865   Refuses to return to the Lycée Saint-Louis and receives private instruction from M. Delzons.

1866   March 7, receives his baccalaureate. April 1, begins his career as a government employee at the Ministry of the Interior. Autumn, enrolls in the Faculties of Law and Letters of the University of Paris and commences his double life as civil servant and law student.

1867   August, passes his first law examination. September 8, M. Jules Og dies. Autumn, Huysmans ventures into journalism and criticism for *La Revue mensuelle*, experiences his first liaison with a soubrette whom he later immortalizes as "Marthe." December, *La Revue mensuelle* ceases publication.

1868   Huysmans continues his liaison with "Marthe" and his employment in the Ministry of the Interior.

1870   July 30, is mobilized with the Garde Nationale Mobile de la Seine at the outbreak of the Franco-Prussian War. September 2, Napoléon III surrenders with his army at Sedan to the Prussians. September 4, the Parisians proclaim a republic in the name of France. Christmas, the Prussians lay siege to Paris.

1871   February, Paris capitulates. Huysmans moves with the National Assembly and the staffs of the government departments to Versailles. Summer, though still employed in the Versailles offices, Huysmans returns to live in Paris.

1872   Recounts his army adventures in a short personal novel entitled *Le Chant du départ*, later to be rewritten as *Sac au dos*.

1874   October 10, publishes *Le Drageoir à épices*, at his own expense, with the House of Dentu.

1875   Publishes essays and art criticism in *Le Musée des Deux Mondes* and in Catulle Mendès' review, *La République des lettres*. Falls under the spell of the Naturalism of Émile Zola.

1876   September 12, publishes *Marthe* in Brussels. Autumn, publishes in the newspaper *L'Actualité*, at Brussels, four important articles under the title *Emile Zola et "L'Assommoir."*

1877   Frequents, among others, the literary company of Émile Zola, Gustave Flaubert, Paul Alexis, Guy de Maupassant, and Edmond and Jules de Goncourt. Regularly publishes his prose poems and critical studies of modern artists in two Belgian reviews: Camille Lemonnier's *L'Actualité* and Théodore Hannon's *L'Artiste*. Simultaneously begins to write *Les Soeurs Vatard*. August 19, *L'Artiste* commences to serialize *Sac au dos*.

1878   July, works on a manuscript entitled *La Faim*.

1879   February 26, publishes *Les Soeurs Vatard*, with Charpentier, and dedicates the novel to Emile Zola. May, becomes art critic of *Le Voltaire* and assesses the Salon of 1879. October 12, publishes his first French edition of *Marthe* with Léon Derveaux. Autumn, frequents the literary circle at Médan. Meets on Sundays with Henry Céard, Léon Hennique, Paul Alexis, and Guy de Maupassant at Émile Zola's villa, twenty miles from Paris.

1880   Contributes *Sac au dos* to the literary collaboration of *Les Soirées de Médan*, a volume of short stories by Zola's circle at Médan. *Sac au dos* differs in several respects from the 1876 version published in *L'Artiste*. Writes a report on the Salon of 1880 for *La Réforme*. Becomes increasingly interested in the Impressionist painters and devotes a critique to the Exposition of the Independents. May 22, publishes *Croquis parisiens*, most of the articles of which have previously appeared in *Le Drageoir aux épices* and in various minor periodicals. Summer, becomes, with Maupassant, a contributor to *Le Gaulois*. Resigns, after his articles on the Jesuits threaten his post at the Ministry of the Interior.

1881 February, publishes *En Ménage*. Publishes *Pierrot sceptique*.

1882 January 26, publishes *A Vau-L'Eau*.

1883 May, publishes a critical study of Impressionism, *L'Art moderne*.

1884 May, publishes *A Rebours*.

1885 August, travels to Lourps to spend several weeks with Anna Meunier, one of her daughters, and her sister Joséphine.

1886 Publishes a new and enlarged edition of *Croquis parisiens*. November, begins to serialize *En Rade* in Édouard Dujardin's *La Revue indépendante*.

1887 April 26, publishes *En Rade* in book form. Publishes *Un Dilemme*.

1888 Summer, travels through Germany in a study of Teutonic art.

1889 Meets Berthe Courrière. November, publishes *Certains*, a collection of articles on art and architecture. Autumn, meets Abbé Joseph-Antoine Boullan.

1890 July, publishes *La Bièvre*, a study of the effect of industry on the Paris river.

1891 Publishes *Là-Bas*. Meets Abbé Arthur Mugnier, who becomes his spiritual advisor.

1892 July, takes his retreat at the Trappist monastery of Notre-Dame d'Igny. August, visits the defrocked Abbé Boullan and his disciples in Lyons.

1893 September 3, becomes a Chevalier of the Légion d'honneur.

1895 February 23, publishes *En Route*.

1896 Begins his intensive study of Chartres Cathedral.

1898 January, publishes *La Cathédrale*. February 16, retires from the Civil Service with the honorary rank of head clerk in the Ministry of the Interior. Publishes *La Bièvre et Saint-Séverin*.

1901 January, publishes *La Bièvre; Les Gobelins; Saint-Séverin*. February 11, publishes *Sainte Lydwine de Schiedam*.

1902 Publishes *De Tout*, a collection of articles. August, publishes *Esquisse biographique sur Don Bosco*.

1903 April, publishes *L'Oblat*.

1905 Publishes *Trois Primitifs, Le Quartier Notre-Dame*. October, goes blind in one eye.

1906 Spring, his physical sufferings increase. September, publishes *Les Foules de Lourdes*. Autumn, his cancer of the mouth and jaw worsens.

1907 May 12, Huysmans dies. May 15, Abbé Mugnier celebrates in the Church of Notre-Dame-des-Champs the requiem mass for Joris-Karl Huysmans, who is buried in the family grave in Montparnasse cemetery.

1908 Posthumous publication of *Trois Églises et Trois Primitifs*.

CHAPTER 1

The Life of the Man

I *His Family and School Days*

HUYSMANS was born on February 5, 1848, in Paris, at No. 11 Rue Suger. He was baptized the very next day under the Christian name of Charles-Marie-Georges. It would be several years before he finally changed his baptismal name to that of Joris-Karl, the Dutch form which he preferred from an early date.

His father, Victor-Godfried-Jan Huysmans, was of Dutch origin. Godfried was born in Breda, Holland, in 1815, and, like several of his ancestors, became a lithographer and designer. During the early Eighteen-Forties he moved to Paris in search of work.

There, in 1845, he met his future wife, Élisabeth-Malvina Badin, a nineteen year old schoolteacher. She, too, shared an artistic tradition, although her father was a cashier in the Ministry of the Interior. She was herself a talented musician and always exhibited an esthetic attitude and appreciation of life.

Daily life in the Huysmans household, from the nuptial day, was singularly uneventful. Young Georges, as he was called in his early years, was already a very taciturn and stubborn child. He generally remained home with his mother, preoccupied with his fantasies and his precocious reading, or, from time to time, went out to play in the Luxembourg Garden. In summer his parents took the boy to visit their relatives in Tilburg or Brussels. Such trips broke the monotony of their mundane existence, and they afforded a certain substance for young Huysmans' limited storehouse of impressions and memories.

Godfried Huysmans, as the years passed, found it increasingly difficult to obtain commissions for his work. He became irascible from repeated failures and from his deteriorating health, as his family lapsed into a kind of genteel poverty. As a consequence, he grew estranged from his wife and their son. Then, suddenly, prematurely, on June 24, 1856, he died.

It was a melancholy autumn. The eight year old Georges began his studies at the Institution Hortus, while his mother, Malvina, remained in mourning. But during the winter she began to receive a male visitor, M. Og, a Protestant by religious faith. They were married, after a whirlwind courtship, in early 1857.

Huysmans, seemingly, never forgave his mother for her impetuous infidelity to the memory of his father. Certainly, too, he never loved his step-father. A year of pain, solitude, and frustration passed for Georges, as, later, so many years of self-imposed isolation were to pass for him, lingeringly, one by one. Still, M. Og provided for his stepson materially, if not with affection. For unlike Godfried Huysmans, M. Og was a businessman with at least a modicum of financial acumen. In May, 1858, for instance, he purchased a book bindery, which he installed on the ground floor of No. 11 Rue de Sèvres, and from which he derived a steady income for years. M. Og continued to provide a comfortable bourgeois existence for his wife and acquired family.

Georges's school years passed in drudgery and unhappiness. In 1862 he left the Institution Hortus and enrolled at the Lycée Saint-Louis. There, rightly or wrongly, though probably with some real justification, he felt mistreated, and even persecuted, by his masters. They baited him, it seems, during his pubescent time of agony. Finally, in 1865, surfeited with real and imagined humiliations, he adamantly refused to return to the lycée. M. and Mme Og surrendered to his wishes after much heated debate. Thus Georges was privately tutored by M. Delzons, one of the masters of the Lycée Saint-Louis, and, in this manner, obtained his baccalaureate diploma on March 7, 1866.

II Early Career and First Love Affair

An intense young manhood began for Georges Huysmans.

Of foremost concern to his family, naturally, was his choice of career. After much discussion, not to say wrangling, Huysmans accepted a post as an *employé de sixième classe* at the Ministry of the Interior. Meanwhile, in his spare time, he was to study law at the University of Paris. So it was that Huysmans assumed his Ministry tasks with perfunctory adequacy, while a single autumn over his books convinced him irrevocably that law could never be his profession, much less his love.

Huysmans confined his hours of leisure to the Latin Quarter. He frequented the cafés and literary circles of the Boulevard Saint-Michel. He encountered the world of contemporary novels, poetry, thought. He became intoxicated with ideas, with new esthetic developments, though he never displayed the slightest interest in or inclination for politics. Most importantly, during this period of his young manhood he discovered the feminine sex.

It was, for him, a shaking discovery.

Huysmans chanced across a lovely young actress one evening at the Théâtre du Luxembourg and promptly fell in love with her, or at least thought he did. It was in remembrance of her, later, that he created the luscious, and vicious, young heroine of his novel *Marthe*. With her he maintained a brief and altogether unsatisfactory liaison, while he wrote theatrical criticism for *La Revue mensuelle* (*The Monthly Review*). Several incidents of the novel closely paralleled certain occurrences of their actual love affair, if such it may be called. But Huysmans, on the whole, chronicled few specific details either in *Marthe* or *Sac au dos* (*Knapsacks*). For one thing, he never mentioned her real name in any of his writing, or even recorded how it was that they separated.

III *Military Experience*

At this time, in what was to become characteristic or perhaps symptomatic misfortune, Huysmans experienced a series of personal losses. First, his stepfather, M. Jules Og, died unexpectedly on September 8, 1867. Second, his mistress, the unknown actress, bore by another lover a child which died almost upon birth, and promptly disappeared from his life with unannounced finality. Third, on the social or political front, war with Prussia broke out in 1870; and Huysmans suddenly found himself, on July 30, inducted to the Garde Nationale de la Seine, on its way to the front lines.

Consequently, it was a time of mournful agony and painful introspection for young Huysmans. Though he never saw military action, he was hospitalized at Châlons from an acute bout with dysentery. No wound could have been more discomfiting or degrading or hardly more serious. Hence, quite ill, he was evacuated westward as the Prussians advanced, and sojourned briefly at Reims, Arras, Évreux. Only the presence of a Catholic nun, Sister

Angèle, of whom he later wrote so affectionately in *Knapsacks,* consoled him during his half-conscious period of convalescence. Here at Évreux, Huysmans received word that Napoleon III had surrendered his entire army at Sedan on September 2, and that a republic had been proclaimed in Paris on September 4. The political turmoil was unimaginable, especially for a budding writer without the slightest predilection for matters political. Huysmans shrugged his shoulders with supreme disinterest and returned home, while France writhed all around him in the most incredible social uproar. Huysmans, nevertheless, was sublimely oblivious of the magnitude of the débâcle and joyfully anticipated a kind of semi-civilian life.

That life waited, for several months, during the siege of Paris from mid-September to the capitulation of the city in February. Huysmans moved with the government to Versailles and thus avoided the revolution of April and May. Still he revealed no concern whatsoever with the deteriorating situation. He simply moved back to his Paris residence that summer, though still employed in the Versailles offices of the Ministry of War.

The war ended with the Prussian victory, of course, and time continued and passed for an intent young man absorbed in reading and fantasies.

IV First Writings

Very little of lasting significance occurred during this time. As far as his personal relationships were concerned, Huysmans became the intimate friend of Ludovic de Vente de Francmesnil, who was also a clerk at the Ministry of War. Ludo, as he was called, shared Huysmans' esthetic predilections and antipathies. It was he who, in 1873, read and marveled over his friend's collection of prose poems, *Le Drageoir à épices* (*The Spice Box*), in their manuscript form. But upon discovering that no commercial publisher seemingly agreed, Huysmans had the book privately printed, in 1874, at the House of Dentu.

Critical apathy toward the book, evidently, disturbed him in no way. Within months Huysmans exhumed the first draft of his war memoirs, *Le Chant du départ,* and re-entitled it *Sac au dos* (*Knapsacks*). He rewrote this short novel, which has become something of a classic, partly from the manuscript of *Le Chant du départ* and partly from his reminiscences of his earlier life and love affair. Meanwhile, his essays and reviews appeared regularly in *Le Musée des Deux-Mondes* and *La République des lettres.*

Huysmans next began work on a longer novel, tentatively entitled *Marthe, histoire d'une fille* (*Martha, the Story of a Prostitute*). The Naturalistic title evidenced the author's desire to depict the life of a harlot in a licensed brothel. It was a rather unusual theme, at least during this stage of literary development, but not really unique. For instance, Huysmans was rather unnerved to discover that Edmond de Goncourt was writing *La Fille Élisa* on the identical subject. Thus Huysmans set to work with redoubled zeal and composed his novel much more rapidly than he anticipated. Quite simply, he wanted to fend off the undesired competition of a firmly established author. Hence, too, it was a race as to which book would be terminated sooner and released first.

So it was that, on August 11, 1876, with time such an important factor, Huysmans left Paris for Brussels in desperate quest of a publisher. He was compelled to accept vanity terms, much to his chagrin, after repeated failures to sign a commercial contract, and subsidized the novel with Callewaert. When finally released to the reading public in September, *Marthe* was by no means a success. The customs officials seized the four hundred copies which Huysmans attempted to take back with him into France. Still, even such police action failed to gain the slightest public interest or even a moderate *succès de scandale.* The entire effect was, simply, to enmesh Huysmans in difficulties with his employers at the Ministry.

It was at this time that Huysmans knotted his friendship with Zola. He also came to know well several other members of the literary group, among them Céard, Hennique, Alexis, and Guy de Maupassant. He quickly absorbed the spirit of Zola's circle and, like the others, rallied to the defense of their common mentor. To this purpose, for instance, Huysmans published in *L'Actualité*, a Brussels newspaper, four articles entitled *Émile Zola et 'L'Assommoir.'* This apologia, when published in booklet form, became one of the most important manifestoes of the Naturalist movement. Furthermore, it cemented his relationship with Émile Zola, who introduced his young protégé to Gustave Flaubert.

It was a fruitful period for Huysmans. He published art criticism and prose poems in Théodore Hannon's *L'Artiste* and Camille Lemonnier's *L'Actualité*. He commenced work on his first long novel, a realistic study, *Les Soeurs Vatard*. And on August 19, 1877, he began serial publication of *Sac au dos* in *L'Artiste*. He was immensely dissatisfied and immediately contemplated a new version, the one which would ultimately appear as his contribution to *Les Soirées de Médan*, a collection of short stories by the various hands of Zola's circle. However, until February 26, 1879, a memorable day of publication for him, Huysmans could think of little other than the novel which consumed him, *Les Soeurs Vatard*, and which, incidentally, he dedicated to his avowed master and the uncontested chieftain of the Naturalist movement, Émile Zola.

It was through this book that Huysmans was assured of a certain notoriety, if not fame. The novel found its audience immediately, and a second printing was released two days after the initial publication. Few critics received the work kindly, much less with praise. The faithful Zola was lavish with encomium, nevertheless, in his sponsorship of his protégé. Undoubtedly, moreover, the very virulence of the critical diatribes afforded Huysmans the benefit of publicity. They ensured *Les Soeurs Vatard* a *succès de scandale*.

V *Hostile Reception by Critics*

For the next two years Huysmans steeped himself more and more deeply in journalism. It was during this period, especially, that he achieved renown as an art critic. He remained busy with the novel, too, for he began *En Ménage* in a spirit of absorption Altogether, it was a very fruitful period.

Huysmans commenced his rôle as critic for *Le Voltaire* with an explosive series of articles. In May, 1879, he penned the first of his twelve articles in that newspaper on the Art Salon of that year. With blithe unconcern for anything but artistic merit, he disregarded almost three thousand canvases. He limited his praise to the smallest handful of unknown painters, like Guillemet and Raffaëlli. Quite expectedly, his championship of the Impressionists and Independents infuriated the public and the art world at large.

It was during this period, too, that Huysmans knotted most

tightly his connections with the Zola circle at Médan. He rewrote and polished still another time the manuscript of his *Sac au dos*, which he included in *Les Soirées de Médan* when it appeared in 1880. As might be expected, *Sac au dos* was the focus of critical attack on account of its supposed obscenity and unpatriotic sentiment. However, none of the authors was perturbed, least of all Huysmans, for the volume of stories had an enormous and unexpected success. In fact, *Les Soirées de Médan* was reprinted no fewer than eight times during its first two weeks of publication.

That same year, in May, the same critics, for the most part, honed their daggers on Huysmans' volume of impressions and prose poems entitled *Croquis parisiens*. For instance, the prose poem, "Le Gousset," a study of the various odors of female armpits, shocked and outraged even Parisian not to say French sensibility. Already the myth of Huysmans as a Decadent writer was beginning to form, albeit somewhat inchoately.

The truth of the matter is that Huysmans counted the hours in the diurnal skein of his extremely tedious existence. He passed his days with the Ministry, his nights with his books and manuscripts. There was little time and almost no money, as legend would later suggest to the contrary, for such Decadent pastimes as the pursuit of women and the quest of succulent dishes. On the sobering level of fact, Huysmans dined inexpensively in bourgeois restaurants, not even well, quite often, and lived something of the *vie manquée* that Flaubert depicted in *L'Éucation sentimentale*. And so his uneventful days passed into uneventful weeks and months, devoid of all excitement but that of cerebration for its own sake.

Such, indeed, was Huysmans' life. Such was the tawdry existence which he described so well with such starkness and such bleak pessimism in *En Ménage*. This novel, published in February, 1881, also met a hostile reception. The critics damned it on moral as well as on literary grounds, and the public at large did not even bother to read it. Commercially the book was something of a failure.

Huysmans was quite discouraged, naturally, but continued to write with dedicated fervor. Immediately he recommenced work on an unfinished manuscript, *La Faim*, but soon abandoned it for *À Vau-l'Eau*. In December, 1881 he sent the manuscript of the brief novel, if that is indeed the proper appellation for it, to the

Kistemaeckers Publishing Company in Brussels. Henry Kistema-eckers, a young man and Huysmans' personal friend, released the work in January, 1882.

A Vau-l'Eau (*Down Stream*), like almost all of Huysmans' other works, met critical disdain as well as public disinterest. This apathy on both parts was to be expected, and it materialized on schedule. This little tale of woe mirrored well enough the daily grief, if not to say diurnal agony, of a minor government function-ary enmeshed in the throes of French bureaucracy. Yet it could hardly excite the sympathetic appreciation of a large audience which had eyes, rather, for the scatological and pornographic novels of the Naturalist school.

Once more, beyond doubt, Huysmans was acutely disap-pointed, if not mortified. Again, too, as so often in the past, he turned to the study of art for consolation. So it was that he col-lected his pieces on the Impressionists and the Independents in a volume of criticism entitled *L'Art moderne* (*Modern Art*), pub-lished by Charpentier in 1883. Reception was, at best, only some-what gratifying to Huysmans. The art world took appropriate no-tice of his work, to be sure, with impassioned polemics for and against his esthetic theses and critical evaluations. But with char-acteristic apathy the public merely ignored the book.

And so time passed, for Huysmans, in literary obscurity.

VI *Fame At Last*

Notoriety, which evolved later into fame, came instantaneously with the publication of *A Rebours* (*Against the Grain*) in 1884. It can be well imagined how this strange, even unique, novel fell, so to speak, like a meteorite among the various journals and news-papers of the day. With few exceptions the professional critics deprecated the book, while painters like Whistler and writers like Bourget, Maupassant, and Gourmont rallied to its defense. Huys-mans' personal friends waxed enthusiastic; Zola alone among them failed to appreciate or even understand the novel. Public reaction was singularly remarkable and almost univocally favor-able. After years of seeking greatness fruitlessly, Huysmans now found thrust upon him literary greatness, or rather fame, when he least anticipated it, and, at that, with the most unexpected of nov-els. At last his reputation was assured and, indeed, secure.

The Life of the Man

It was Barbey d'Aurevilly who, more than any other critic, seized the essence of the novel. In *Le Constitutionnel* he compared *A Rebours* to Baudelaire's *Fleurs du mal* (*Flowers of Evil*). With admirable acumen and flashing insight into the future, Barbey observed:

Baudelaire, the satanic Baudelaire, who died a Christian, must surely be one of M. Huysmans' favourite authors, for one can feel his presence, like a glowing fire, behind the finest pages M. Huysmans has written. Well, one day, I defied Baudelaire to begin *Les Fleurs du mal* over again, or to go any further in his blasphemies. I might well offer the same challenge to the author of *A Rebours*. "After *Les Fleurs du mal*," I told Baudelaire, "it only remains for you to choose between the muzzle of a pistol and the foot of the Cross." Baudelaire chose the foot of the Cross. But will the author of *A Rebours* make the same choice? [1]

Already apparent from all Huysmans' writing, thus, was his inevitable decision, his conversion, or, rather, his return to the bosom of the Church.

The year 1884 was memorable not only for the publication of *A Rebours* but also for a marked change in Huysmans' personal friendships. His relationship with Zola degenerated perceptibly, almost to the point of collapse, while he began an intimate association with Léon Bloy. During that summer, too, he visited his favorite vacation village, Jutigny. Once again he worked on his still unfinished novel, *La Faim* (*Hunger*), but soon abandoned the project. At the same time, with Bloy, he knotted his friendship with Villiers de l'Isle-Adam, who was to play an increasingly important rôle in his life.

Time passed.

Huysmans began to write *En Rade* (*At Harbor*). But he was still composing the work in November, 1886 when Édouard Dujardin started to serialize it for *La Revue indépendante* (*The Independent Review*). Simultaneously from this time dated his heated discussions with his friends, including Bloy and Villiers, over literature, music, and other esthetic matters, and particularly over his seeming lack of appreciation for Wagner's music, which was then the rage in Decadent circles.

En Rade was published as a book in 1887. But like all his other novels except *A Rebours*, it at once encountered an indifferent if not hostile audience. Huysmans thought, perhaps erroneously, that the tepid reception was due in part to the limited publicity afforded by his new publisher, Stock. At least Charpentier, his former publisher, had always been able to produce, and thus guarantee, a kind of public curiosity through the very virulence of critics whom he had baited and provoked to this end. Perhaps, too, Huysmans had grown addicted to a public adulation, which would never really be his again, from the resounding success accorded *A Rebours*. Yet he managed to soothe his frustration with an interest, albeit a forced one, in the scenes of the surrounding countryside and particularly in the baroque aspects of the Château de Lourps.

VII *Friendship and Travels*

It should never be thought that Huysmans was a solitary without friends. He was known, rather, as a good host and a good friend. In his circle at No. 11 Rue de Sèvres, limited though it was, he entertained and aided, as best he could, Georges Landry and Henri Girard. He also received Lucien Descaves, who, years later, would prove to be his finest commentator, editor, and executor. He even knew and cultivated the erratic Paul Verlaine. Still, his dearest friend, and in a sense his literary favorite, was Villiers de l'Isle-Adam.

At the same time Huysmans ceased to be close to Zola, and he no longer frequented the literary circles of Paris. Such milieus were much too organized for him. Sporadically, instead, he saw fellow writers like Mallarmé and visited editors like Édouard Dujardin of *La Revue indépendante*. He limited himself to a few soirées at the Goncourts'. His friendships, though, were perfunctory and lukewarm. Indeed, his post at the Ministry of the Interior absorbed his days; and his novels, criticism, and occasional prose poems occupied his all too few hours of leisure. Huysmans, at this time, was never really intimate with anyone.

In the summer of 1888, Huysmans, who had more inclination than opportunity for travel, decided to visit several of the more famous German cathedrals. He wanted to study their religious art.

Hence, in August, he took a train to Cologne, where he intended to spend some time at the great cathedral. From there he left for the Hanseatic cities, particularly Lübeck and Hamburg. He was unfavorably impressed by Berlin, the museum of which he nonetheless admired, but intrigued by Weimar, Erfurt, and Gotha. After such esthetic exhilaration Huysmans experienced a profound spell of depression upon his return to Paris.

This depression continued and grew even profounder during 1889. He saw very little of Bloy, who had developed into one of his closest friends. Moreover, Villiers de l'Isle-Adam was fatally ill with cancer, which consumed him for month after month of unimaginably excruciating pain. Finally, on August 18, death came as his ultimate release; and Villiers de l'Isle-Adam was buried on August 21. To the end, at every free moment, Huysmans had remained faithfully by his side.

Huysmans' melancholia deepened perceptibly from the experience.

VIII *Berthe*

It was in the year 1889, too, through Remy de Gourmont, at his apartment, that Huysmans first encountered the strange woman who would soon play such an important rôle in his life. She was named Caroline-Louise-Victoire Courrière, or, more simply, Berthe, as her friends called her. She had already been the mistress of the sculptor Clésinger, her "uncle." Now she was living with her "cousin," Remy de Gourmont, the brilliant young writer. It seems, indeed, that Mme Courrière ran through a singular array of "uncles" and "cousins" throughout the literary circles of Paris.

Immediately Huysmans was drawn to Mme Courrière. The preceding year, in 1888, he had become the lover of Henriette Maillat, who whetted his latent interest in occultism; and this interest grew immeasurably during the following years of their sporadic liaison. Now he felt the most intense physical attraction for the beautiful and mysterious Berthe Courrière. As his relationship with her continued and deepened, his concern with mysticism, furthermore, became an obsession. The principal difference between his two mistresses, incidentally, is that whereas Henriette preferred authors, Berthe Courrière specialized, so to speak, in men of the Church. It was to prove a dangerous specialty, indulged in compulsively. Thus her interest in Huysmans was natural. He was already a distinguished writer, and very shortly thereafter he was to become something of a man of the Church. Both aspects of his personality exerted an irresistible appeal upon her.

IX Satanism and the Occult

Huysmans' preoccupation with the occult was initially esthetic. It began innocuously enough with his study of Gustave Moreau's art and progressed through his essays on the Sataniques of Félicien Rops. Hereupon he immediately deepened his interest in satanism through his biography of Gilles de Rais, who was a notorious diabolist of the Middle Ages.

So it was that with quickened interest Huysmans began to frequent the satanist groups of Paris. He often traveled to Belgium, especially to Brussels. He made several pilgrimages to Lyons, which was then, at least by reputation, the capital of European satanism. Subsequently he was involved in several scandals with religious, or rather sacrilegious, overtones, notably in connection with the Abbé Louis Van Haecke, whom he considered the Gilles de Rais of the nineteenth century. Moreover, his lady friends, especially Berthe Courrière, involved him, almost criminally, in certain unsavory episodes which more than smacked of licentious diabolism.

Worse was still to come. In the closing months of 1889, Huysmans first heard of an infamous defrocked priest, Joseph-Antoine Boullan, who was to play a certain nefarious rôle in his life, and whose diabolical practices were by repute the most flagrantly sinister of modern times in all France. At Bellevue, near Paris, in the religious community which he founded, he maintained a notorious liaison with Sister Adèle Chevalier. In this connection there were numerous rumors of his many spiritual impurities, of his desecrated hosts, and of the actual human sacrifice of his own child by Sister Adèle upon the very altar of God. Such rumors were rife, indeed, and, in some cases, either unfounded or exaggerated beyond belief. Yet many of the most outrageous tales of satanistic practice proved to be, in time, only too true.

Hence it was that many complaints were repeatedly filed against him with both the police and the Church. Perhaps many of them were false, and certainly most of them were never sub-

stantiated for lack of evidence. Yet the total effect of the whisper-
ing campaign against him, with its distorted fact and innuendo,
gathered and even spread by the police and the Church, was
overwhelmingly detrimental in the sheer weight of its scandal.

In February, 1890, Huysmans discovered how intimate the relations of Berthe Courrière had been with the ex-Abbé Boullan.
Thus his curiosity was further aroused, although a recent acquaintance, Oswald Wirth, attempted to dissuade him from meeting the defrocked priest. Undaunted, Huysmans struck up a
correspondence with Boullan, who at that time resided in Lyons.

With consuming interest Huysmans received Julie Thibault,
who was Boullan's priestess-housekeeper, upon her visit to the
writer in Paris. Hence, too, he began to write at length, in thinly
disguised form, about his subject, the modern Gilles de Rais, the
infamous diabolist, Boullan, whom he had still not met in the
flesh. His writing, of course, assumed the form of a novel entitled
Là-Bas (*Down There*), which would shortly prove to be one of
his most popular and enduring works. It was through the compo-
sition of the novel, and particularly through the influence of Boullan, that Huysmans definitively acquired, and even maintained, a
healthy respect for supernatural matters.

X *A Spiritual Crisis*

So it was that Huysmans' life began to change perceptibly. He
rapidly approached a spiritual crisis which had been coming to a
head for years. For part of his basic "research" on *La Bièvre et
Saint-Séverin,* he had often consorted with both prostitutes and
criminals in the most ignominious sections of Paris. His association with them, or at least his proximity to them, left an indelible
imprint upon his character. This imprint, so to speak, formed a
certain trait of the most salient aspect of his "decadent" personality.

Now Huysmans revealed a radically different aspect of his
character. He began to experience a profound sense of the religious impulse. Suddenly, inexplicably, one morning his was the
faith which he had sought so long so fruitlessly. It came to him,
unexpectedly, at the moment he least hoped for it, as the free gift
of a merciful God. He felt cleansed by saving grace.

Immediately his "new" religious consciousness, although amply foreshadowed in previous work, colored his writing. Still, all but his most intimate friends regarded his conversion, or, rather, his spiritual awakening, as an involuted reflection of his esthetic penchant for Decadent religiosity. His Catholicism, they assumed erroneously, was specious, not sincere, with his devotion being to that of mere ritual and ceremonial rather than to God.

His critics were wrong.

As he sought to conform to the precept of chastity, Huysmans was sorely tempted by the demon of the flesh. He freely admitted this. After all, he had long been an addict to carnal pleasures, or so he thought of himself. So, now that he no longer possessed Anna Meunier or Henriette Maillat, he once more began to frequent brothels whenever he could resist temptation no longer. A beautiful prostitute named Fernande, in particular, intrigued him. He repeatedly tried to disentangle himself from her bewitchment, but to no avail. On her account, he suffered the agonies of many a struggle between conscience and the devil. To his credit, nonetheless, he gradually, though most painfully and after much struggle, won his ultimate victory.

For this reason Huysmans sought to enlist the aid of a spiritual director. At Berthe Courrière's suggestion he contacted a priest whom she knew, a certain Léonce de Saint-Paul; but to his surprise the latter summarily rejected him. His efforts to find a suitable confessor went unrewarded for some time.

At length, again through Mme Courrière's solicitude, Huysmans made the acquaintance of the Abbé Arthur Mugnier. The occasion was on Thursday evening, May 28, 1891; the place, the sacristy of Saint-Thomas-d'Aquin. The writer fell upon his knees there, and entreated the priest for spiritual succor, or, rather, as he said, for chlorine for his soul.

Immediately Huysmans and the Abbé Mugnier liked each other. During the coming years their predilection was to wax into a close friendship. Their association, indeed, would go far beyond the mere bounds of a spiritual counselor giving advice to a penitent sinner returned to the bosom of the Church.

At once, Huysmans threw down his psychic gauntlet and, in a sense, declared holy war upon the wily devil. It was a duello, a fight to the death. Thus he commenced his diurnal exercises of moral control in a conscious effort to strengthen his will and to develop his conscience. Thus he would perfect himself, he thought, in his daily struggle against the forces of evil. It was with this intent and with this purpose in mind that he frequently called upon Abbé Mugnier. Yet, at the same time, he continued to receive detailed instruction in magic and related subjects from the singularly disreputable Abbé Boullan. The two aspects of his religious being hardly seemed compatible to some observers.

Huysmans scrupulously carried out all the forms demanded by the Catholic faith with a characteristic determination. In the meanwhile, he waited and prayed for his moment of truth. There came, in June, 1892, the apogee of his spiritual crisis, i.e., his true "repentance," or the willful rejection of his old Adamic life. He was shaken to the innermost core of his being. For the first time he thought seriously about entering a religious house.

In response to his pointed query the Abbé Mugnier suggested as particularly suitable for a person of his contemplative mood the Trappist monastery of Notre-Dame d'Igny, near Fismes. It was there, for a week, that Huysmans took his retreat. Loaded down with a heavy portmanteau of his spiritual and physical necessities, he presented himself to Father Léon on July 12. More than ever, he was determined to pursue the spiritual bout to the end and to confront God Himself before he left.

His sojourn at the monastery was one of the most deeply meaningful experiences of his life. Certainly, too, it was a turning-point, for despite momentary lapses of the flesh he would never return to his former ways. Notre-Dame d'Igny became, very rapidly, the battlefield where he developed into a hardened veteran. Living the Christian life, in harmony with God's holy laws, was that difficult for him.

His nine days of silence, solitude, and spiritual solace were eternally fateful for Huysmans. From his notes it seems that he suffered a kind of nervous breakdown during that period of profound reflection and examination. But whereas the interminable days of this self-immolating isolation were, in truth, agonizing, his physical health, at least, was greatly improved during his retreat. He emerged the victor. He emerged triumphant from the self-confrontation in his quest of God.

Upon his return to Paris, Huysmans found that he could tolerate the hustle and noise of the megalopolis for only three days.

The city was too much for him in his new mood. Then, still impelled by his obsessive craving for solitude, he departed for a visit of a fortnight in Lyons. He took with him the stoical habits which he had acquired at the monastery. Each day he arose very early and spent the mornings strolling along the Rhône. He ate sparingly. He spent most of his time alone in reflection. He also visited, of course, all the city's churches and convents.

His sojourn in Lyons also afforded him the opportunity to immerse himself more deeply in his studies of magic and of demonology. To this end he met Abbé Boullan every day, generally at lunch, and engaged him in long and fruitful conversations about occult matters. Huysmans listened well and learned much. He admired and liked immensely the Abbé Boullan, despite the latter's unsavory and even infamous reputation.

"Scandal" broke, so to speak, while Huysmans was in Lyons. On July 30, *Le Figaro* reported the rumor that the Naturalist writer, who had evolved into a Decadent, had now embraced the Catholic faith in a dramatic conversion at a Trappist monastery. Devout Catholics and popular novelists alike were astounded by the news that the most seemingly unlikely of men had suddenly become a Christian believer.

Understandably, Huysmans, for his part, was both annoyed by the journalistic invasion of his privacy and afraid for his post as a civil servant. Anti-clericalism was still strong in France. Hence, he immediately wrote the editor of *Le Figaro* to deny that he had ever taken a retreat anywhere. Tempers flared momentarily since few believed that the "conversion," if indeed it had taken place, was sincere. But they soon subsided in a spirit of general reconciliation. The entire episode had dissipated by the time Huysmans returned to Paris in mid-August.

Upon his return to Paris, Huysmans received the Abbé Mugnier. After his recent experiences, spiritually intoxicating as they were, there was quite naturally a great deal for him to discuss with his confessor. Certainly, via Notre-Dame d'Igny and Lyons, Huysmans had emerged a radically changed man.

XI *Personal Tragedy and Suffering*

At once Huysmans set about the task of writing a novel which assimilated his religious experiences. In it he presented a broken and contrite Durtal, who had recently been converted to Catholicism, and who had recently made his first retreat to a Trappist monastery. For his research on the work he amassed a mountain of notes on Church art, liturgy, and related subjects. But he spent most of his days in close conversation with various friends, priests, who helped him thresh out the many theological difficulties inherent in this account, thinly fictionalized, of a young writer's intense spiritual crisis.

In the autumn and the winter of 1892, Huysmans worked upon his novel with great contentment. During this period of literary fertility he often received the Abbé Boullan, who often came to Paris under an assumed name expressly to see him. Huysmans derived much intellectual benefit and mystical gratification from these visits. Unfortunately, however, they were cut short by a sudden and unforeseeable tragedy. The Abbé Boullan died in Lyons, most unexpectedly, on January 3, 1893. Huysmans was stunned and incapacitated for days over his profound and abiding sense of personal loss. He would always feel the immense void left by the untimely demise of his mentor in occultism.

Yet another tragedy, a deep personal loss, followed several weeks later. His former mistress, Anna Meunier, always of unsteady mental health, had grown increasingly psychotic; or so the symptoms seemed. In fact, her general situation became quite desperate. Huysmans himself had to commit her to Sainte-Anne, although she was immediately transferred to Villejuif after several weeks of observation and then back to Sainte-Anne. Her pitiable incarceration seemed, for a while, more or less permanent.

So it was that, more than ever, Huysmans turned to religious introspection for solace. His losses, naturally, weighed heavily upon him, particularly since he had always been something of an introvert. Furthermore, his physical health, which had always been rather bad, now worsened perceptibly. He suffered from a chronic neurasthenia. His pain contributed, undoubtedly, to the difficulties which he invariably experienced in all his personal relationships. His numerous ailments and illnesses tortured him psychologically. To a certain extent, as he was the first to realize, they even twisted his spiritual development, at least for a while. Yet, in all his pain, suffering, and solitude, he had no presentiment of the physical agonies through which he would have to pass one day, when his body, racked by pain, approached its final hours. Death would come to him as blessed relief from physical suffering.

XII *Projects for Spiritual Retreats*

In summer, 1893, with the weight of his literary efforts and the onus of official duties heavy upon him, Huysmans decided to make another retreat at La Trappe. There, again, he found and applied to a worn soul his spiritual balm of contemplation and solitude. There, as he said later, he scrubbed his soul until it felt clean again. He was a man in love with spiritual purity.

It was an auspicious period of life. On September 3, Huysmans became a Chevalier de la Légion d'honneur. However, sadly enough, it was not the brilliant writer whom the government honored with the award of its coveted decoration. It was, rather, the faithful civil servant who had already spent twenty-seven long years, almost to his disbelief, in the government service. He was shocked to realize that he had already grown so advanced in years. The award, then, was for him something of a traumatically self-conscious occasion.

The otherwise uneventful year passed. During the interval he became increasingly aware of his intense dissatisfaction with the bureaucratic life. He began to daydream of retiring and of devoting himself to fiction, art criticism, and religion, particularly to the religious life. His fondest vision was that of an ideal life, during his declining years, in an artistic monastery, completely isolated, totally absorbed in spiritual and esthetic contemplation.

So it was that, in this frame of mind, Huysmans decided to visit Saint-Wandrille. He wanted to make a basilica of the arts from this ancient abbey, which had pathetically fallen into ruin. It became an obsessive dream during those July days when he examined it for the first time. He remained there for a week of pleasant reflection and ecstatic investigation of all details. He was confident that he had found an avocation for life. Yet, by Sunday, July 8, somewhat to his saddened realization, he had already lost his excitement over the restoration.

Again Huysmans turned his thoughts to La Trappe, as he invariably did whenever he felt his interest in a project drain away. His ecstatic reminiscences of Igny were to prove now, as ever after, the solace and the passion of his life. He hesitated, nonetheless, as he frequently did, and contented himself with the idealized dream of La Trappe rather than with its concrete reality.

Huysmans returned to Paris and resumed his work with an ache of discontent. Saint-Wandrille was especially a subject of despair for him. Meanwhile, he was overwhelmed by another personal tragedy. His beloved former mistress, Anna Meunier, died at Sainte-Anne on February 12, 1895. Her loss crushed him.

More difficulty loomed upon the horizon, this time in the guise of literature. His most recent novel, *En Route,* which was published by Stock on February 23, was relentlessly assailed by the critics. Yet certain perspicacious observers, among whom was Paul Valéry, were unstinting in their praise.

Public response, however, was surprisingly favorable. Quite rapidly *En Route* went through several editions. Huysmans, of course, was elated by the general acclaim. Nevertheless, he was irritated by a flood of mail from unknown correspondents, who plagued him with countless questions about spiritualism and religion. With his typical conscientiousness he tried to answer as many of the letters as possible.

Shortly thereafter, Huysmans commenced another novel, to be entitled *La Cathédrale.* Once more his hero was Durtal; and his subject, this time, was the effect of medieval art and architecture upon his spiritual development. The locale, or secondary subject, was Chartres, with all its beauty, majesty, mystery. As always Huysmans enjoyed his work immensely, for he had a predilection for such matter.

In the spring and summer of 1895, Huysmans was frequently interrupted. Almost all his visitors, like Édouard Dubus, an ostensible victim of diabolical possession, came to call upon the writer as a kind of spiritual duty. Then, too, as ever, there were the devout Catholics who came to pay their homage to a great and often misunderstood author of Christian piety and mysticism.

Hence, with such excessive activity filling his life, Huysmans reflected upon the harmony and order of the monastic life. On July 1, Huysmans left Paris with Boucher and the Abbé Ferret for a retreat in the Abbey of Fiancey in southern France. They visited clerical friends along the way. They were exhausted by the time they arrived at Fiancey. However, he was soon to cleanse and to refresh his soul, as he had hoped. His retreat, this time, was an extremely happy one. He returned to Paris later, via Dijon, where he spent two days, with Boucher but without the Abbé Ferret.

That winter Huysmans was a frequent traveler to Chartres. That Christmas, too, following his custom, he attended midnight mass in the crypt. He was, in retrospect, both dissatisfied and content at the same time, for another year, a typical year in his advancing life, i.e., one meaningful without being eventful, had passed.

Friendship became increasingly important for Huysmans as he grew older. The year 1896 was particularly noteworthy in this respect. In April he knotted his ties with two men who, in time, became perhaps his dearest friends. The first was the Abbé Mugnier, who was the sophisticated curate of Sainte-Clotilde. The second was Lucien Descaves, who was an intensely masculine and anti-clerical ex-soldier. As the year developed, Huysmans met and came to admire a number of other men and even some women. He had changed direction, indeed, from the painful isolation of his earlier life.

In July Huysmans applied for another leave of absence from the ever indulgent Ministry so that he might return to his spiritual home at Notre-Dame d'Igny. His request was approved. He found the monastery, as he later reported to the Abbé Mugnier, to be radically changed. It was now a place of comparative luxury. At least, the former austerity was greatly modified. Hours of meditation were shorter, leisure was more available, and there was a far wider selection of foods.

Huysmans, understandably, felt refreshed upon his return to Paris. Still, Igny had now lost something of its charm for him. Now he thought of a peaceful retirement to Saint-Pierre de Solesmes even more than at Saint-Wandrille. Instead of going there, however, he visited Chartres. His life, certainly, had been increasingly circumscribed by monasteries and cathedrals. Their itinerary told his days, so to speak, like the beads of a rosary.

XIII *More Tragedy and Relief in Travel*

The death of another friend cast a long shadow over Huysmans. The Abbé Ferret expired of cancer in 1897. Moreover, Charles Buet, the Catholic writer portrayed as Chantelouve in *Là-Bas*, was buried in April of that year. Huysmans, furthermore, had estranged certain of his friends, notably Stéphane Mallarmé, over misunderstandings about occult matters. It was always to prove a thorny subject of debate.

So it happened that Huysmans, through long contemplation of the melancholy fate of his close friend, the Abbé Ferret, became more and more absorbed in the idea of death and human suffering. In this lugubrious frame of mind he started on his next work, *Sainte Lydwine de Schiedam* (*Saint Lydwine of Schiedam*), a study in hagiography. Thus, too, in quest of background material, he traveled to Belgium and Holland with his friends, the Leclaires. He enjoyed himself immensely and recorded many of his impressions of the various cities. Travel was a most welcome relief after the overwhelming sense of loss which he had so recently experienced over the deaths of so many of his closest friends.

XIV *Retirement and Life as an Oblate*

One of the major events of Huysmans' life occurred on February 16, for then he retired from the Civil Service with the honorary rank of head clerk.

At first, Huysmans hardly knew how to utilize all the free time which he found readily accessible. The days were long and heavy. Literature, whether by his reading or through his writing, could not fill all the tedious hours. Thus, soon, he began to suffer from anxiety.

In his acute loneliness Huysmans began to ruminate about women. More than ever, now that age closed in upon him, he wished that he had married as a young man and reared a family. Marriage, after all, was a sacrament of the Church; and now he yearned for it. A wife would have provided the companionship which he had always sought but which he had never found. She would also have counteracted the demon of the flesh, from which he suffered so acutely at the time. Indeed, now, at midsummer, with his life more than half over, his fifty years weighed heavily upon him, although he was famous, financially independent, and at his cultivated ease.

He searched, almost desperately, for projects to while away the hours.

In July 1898, somewhat reluctantly, he decided to visit Solesmes. His sojourn there was a struggle against the bewitching seductiveness of an absent woman, the Countess de Galoez. She even threatened, by correspondence, to call upon him, within the very walls of the monastery, if need be, with or without his consent, and tempt him to sacrilege before the very altar of the crucified and risen Lord. Surely, from the trauma of this almost incredible episode, the saintly writer reflected upon his earlier difficulties with women and relished the debilitation of his aging body, now that such carnal demands no longer compelled him to betray both God and his better judgment.

Upon his return to Paris, during the following months, Huysmans busied himself with two projects. The first was to rid himself of the very attractive but unwanted Countess de Galoez. In this he succeeded only after much real effort and many stratagems. The second task, which was far more important, was to construct a new home for himself at Ligugé. This activity he pursued with evident relish.

There, at Ligugé, Huysmans was supremely happy. There, too, certain of his friends traveled to visit him. He received them, in his literary court, with his characteristic grace, charm, and solicitude. He enjoyed the rôle of literary lion. He enjoyed his leisure. He enjoyed the companionship of his friends. Indeed, in his new home, creating a new atmosphere, he was rapidly mellowing, even to his own surprise.

In March, 1900, Huysmans became a Benedictine oblate. He was overjoyed by the habit of the new life and entered the spirit of the monastery with heady anticipation. Thus he was saddened by a called meeting of the Académie Goncourt, of which he was the oldest member, for the election of three academicians. Literature was to interest him less and less. Hence, sickened of Paris, disenchanted by literary manipulations, he dashed back to Ligugé in time for the paschal dinner. This holy meal always meant a great deal to him.

The remainder of the year passed uneventfully. Huysmans alternated between Ligugé and the monastery, between literature and the spiritual life. Then, on December 31, 1900, he entered the new century, which, he realized with foreboding, would always seem foreign to a nineteenth-century man like himself. He experienced a deep sense of malaise.

The Life of the Man

In 1901 Huysmans resumed his rôle as man of letters and published two books. In January he released *La Bièvre; Les Gobelins; Saint-Séverin* through the Société de Propagation des Livres d'Art in an illustrated, limited edition. During the summer he published *Sainte Lydwine de Schiedam,* which quickly provoked much controversy. He admitted, later, that he was profoundly dissatisfied with the finished work in question.

On March 21, Huysmans solemnly professed himself as a Benedictine oblate. He assumed "John" as his name in religion. Again dropping all literary concerns, he found a time of happiness in his spiritual contemplation.

In June Huysmans returned to Paris. Then he visited Dijon to gather material for his next novel, *L'Oblat* (*The Oblate*). The trip fatigued him. His home at Ligugé exercised upon him an irresistible appeal.

In December, shortly before Christmas, Huysmans commenced the actual writing of *L'Oblat.* It was to be the third novel of his Catholic trilogy. He was eager to terminate the work. Yet, two months later, he set the novel aside for a while, in order to devote himself exclusively to another essay in hagiography, *Esquisse biographique sur Don Bosco* (*Biographical Sketch of Don Bosco*).

XV Deteriorating Health

Winter passed, and spring, without incident, except for a grave case of pneumonia. There was a single event of importance during the summer. Huysmans visited Marseilles to meet a mysterious and hitherto unknown Dr. Rodaglia. The details of the imbroglio were not important. What mattered, from Huysmans' standpoint, was that, once again, he would retain, and entertain, indelible impressions of another encounter with the occult.

On August 7, 1902, in Paris, Huysmans left his old quarters on the Rue Monsieur for his new apartment on the Rue de Babylone. He was delighted. Over the years, certainly, he had been, for the most part, quite unhappy in the Rue Monsieur. Physical surroundings were always important to his literary creativity.

On September 10, Huysmans joined the Abbé Mugnier in a visit to Notre-Dame-de-la-Treille at Lille. From there he traveled to Bruges for the 1902 Exhibition of Primitives. He had never quite lost his interest in art, but he no longer possessed his youthful enthusiasm for the subject. At any rate, this exhibition, he felt, was definitely an esthetic disappointment.

Huysmans felt another friend, though no longer an intimate one, slip away in September. For it was then that his former mentor, Émile Zola, died. Huysmans, of course, was much saddened because of the affectionate memories which he still retained of the man who had given him aid, advice, and inspiration. He did not attend the funeral, however, because of the political demonstrations which he felt certain would materialize. He simply forced himself to forget Zola's death and continued to work on *L'Oblat*.

In 1903 Huysmans discovered the profound meaning of the holy spectacles of Lourdes. He was so fascinated as to be almost hypnotized by the great pilgrimages of autumn. Yet he was unstinting in his criticism of the physical ugliness which, he felt, afflicted much of the environs.

In September Huysmans accompanied the Abbé Mugnier on a sightseeing tour in Germany and Belgium. On their roll-call of cities were Strasbourg, Frankfurt-am-Main, Cologne, Brussels, and Antwerp. As ever, Huysmans prowled about the older sections of each city and investigated every cathedral in sight. He returned to Paris with a veritable storehouse of impressions.

Huysmans' physical health worsened perceptibly. His jaw ached frightfully from a disease which would later be diagnosed as cancer. Perhaps his emotional well-being, too, degenerated somewhat. By January, 1904, he felt that he was being pursued by evil spirits.

On March 1, 1904, Huysmans moved to an apartment on the Rue Sainte-Placide. The rooms were spacious and sunny, and they would evidently afford him innumerable hours of pleasure and relaxation. The move took his mind off the intolerable pain in his jaw. Perhaps he moved to his new quarters, this time, with the half-conscious realization that this home would be his last.

And so it was to be.

That very day *Le Mois littéraire et pittoresque* (*The Month in Literature and Art*) published the first essay of his *Trois Primitifs* (*Three Primitives*), i.e., "Les Grünewald du Musée de Colmar" ("The Grünewald Paintings of the Colmar Museum"). More noteworthy, however, were two important prefaces which almost immediately gained fame for him. The first was his preface to a new

edition of *A Rebours,* published by the Société des Cent Biblio-
philes, in which he explained the rôle of the novel in his development and how it vitally contributed to his spiritual conversion.
The second was his explicatory and evaluative preface to Paul
Verlaine's *Poésies religieuses* (*Spiritual Poems*). His choice of
subject and treatment both revealed his undying interest in religious matters.

Huysmans began to make frequent pilgrimages to Lourdes.
Perhaps his rapidly deteriorating health motivated him somewhat
to visit the locale of so many miraculous cures. In the meanwhile,
he worked busily upon his latest book, *Les Deux Faces de
Lourdes* (*The Two Faces of Lourdes*). Stock was to publish the
work in October, but suddenly the author went blind in one eye.
He was forced to bed as he was assailed by a plethora of other
ailments. Winter and spring passed in unspeakable physical
agony. Not until April could he resume work on the book, now
entitled *Les Foules de Lourdes* (*The Crowds of Lourdes*). The
book was published in September, 1906, and sold seventeen thousand copies during the first month.

In December Huysmans suffered an operation and the removal
of nearly all his teeth. By January, realizing that he did not have
much longer to live, Lucien Descaves and Gustave Geffroy, his
friends, persuaded Aristide Briand, the Minister of Public Instruction, to promote him to the rank of Officer de la Légion
d'honneur in recognition of his literary accomplishments. Huysmans, of course, was singularly gratified, particularly in view of
the vehement attacks brought against him by the left-wing press.

The end was near.

XVI   *Last Days*

Huysmans was ravaged by cancer of the jaw. He could no
longer leave his bed, even for short intervals. He was further
weakened by fever. His few remaining teeth were extracted. The
cancer spread rapidly. He suffered a severe hemorrhage on April
21. On April 23 he received from the Abbé Fontaine the sacrament of Extreme Unction.

Huysmans was now horribly disfigured. Yet, as a devout and
stoical Christian, he received his friends with strained cordiality.

He struggled on. He carefully arranged all his manuscripts and papers while suffering almost unbelievable pain.

On May 12, 1907 Huysmans died quietly in his room. On May 15 the Abbé Mugnier celebrated for him, as he had requested, a requiem mass at the Church of Notre-Dame-des-Champs. Huysmans was buried, then, at the Montparnasse cemetery in the family grave. A light rain fell as he was lowered to his eternal rest.

CHAPTER 2

The Naturalist

I A Dish of Spices

IT is singular, indeed, that Huysmans, as a young civil servant who never even experiences a "naturalist" life, should commence his first period of literary creativity, the so-called Naturalist period, with the publication of a book of Decadent prose poems. But so he does. It is immediately apparent, therefore, that Huysmans is far too complex to be neatly categorized, even during any single time-span of his life. Yet, while the classifications are more specious than actual, they can at least serve a useful function. They are a convenient signpost in pointing out the general direction pursued by the writer during a certain period of his life.

The little volume of prose poems in question is entitled *Le Drageoir à épices*, later modified as *Le Drageoir aux épices* (translated as *A Dish of Spices*), which the author first published at Paris with Dentu in 1874, under the name of Jorris-Karl Huysmans. With the second edition of the book, the following year, he forever changed the spelling of his Christian name, *Jorris*, to that of *Joris*, which he had come to prefer. There were no other textual changes.

A Dish of Spices is a youthful work, which bears the obvious imprint of earlier specialists in the prose poem, like Aloysius Bertrand and Charles Baudelaire. Huysmans' prose poems, like theirs, are highly imagistic, involuted, and often contrived. Several of them are quite tortured, so to speak, even to the point of awkwardness; and in terms of value they do not approximate the work of Bertrand, much less Baudelaire. However, some of them recall Théophile Gautier's *tours de force* and are little mosaics composed of infinitesimal *bric-à-brac*.

There is a danger in such writing. It strives too often to reach an apogee, an intensity, a pitch which either cannot be attained or cannot be long maintained. The most cursory reading of *A Dish of*

Spices reveals this fact. In "Japanese Rococo," for instance, Huysmans tortures himself in purple prose as he writes to his beloved of fantasy:

I love, O cajoling she-wolf, the miaulings of your voice; I love your ululating and raucous tones; but I love above all, I could die of love for, your nose, your little nose, which escapes from the folds of your loosened hair like a yellow rose blowing in black foliage.[1]

This kind of writing is so evidently forced that it borders upon the ludicrous. Moreover, this kind of writing, of similar quality, predominates in the book.

Still, when he does not hook one sentence on to another in a state of exotic frenzy, Huysmans can pen a felicitous phrase upon occasion. Even here, in his earliest efforts, he is by no means an execrable writer. For example, he describes a strikingly lovely woman in "Red Cameo":

The all-powerful goddess was hidden in the cushions of the divan, flicking her red tresses against the cerise satin, unfurling her rose petticoat and twirling, on the end of her foot her tiny morocco slipper. She sighed daintily, arose, stretched her arms, snapped her joints, seized a big-bellied bottle and poured into a little glass, tapering of stem and shaped like a gimlet, a filament of reddish-brown port.[2]

This is not an immortal passage of great literature, by any means; nor is it even particularly distinguished. But the writer does evidence an admirable feeling for words, and the passage could well come from one of the more Decadent works of the *fin de siècle*. Huysmans does mold a certain Decadent beauty through his imagistic diction.

Such a flavor often prevails in this collection of prose poems. Such thematic material, too, is most often the subject matter. For instance, in "Declaration of Love," which is transparently inspired by Baudelaire, the poet addresses his beloved Ninon, and reproaches her for her compulsion to wallow in sexual mire, while at the same time confessing that he loves her all the more for her self-destructive tendencies. Their relationship exemplifies, admirably well, the familiar Decadent theme of the reversal of the rôles in love. This motif is further evidenced by "Claudine," who, as a modern woman, is by definition a sado-masochist. "Cowardice" is a story of an effeminate man, a "panty-waist," who fawns before a sadistic and faithless woman. Here, as usual, love is perverted. Hence, too, in "La Reine Margot" a delicate young woman rejects her tender and wealthy suitor, so that she can find carnal pleasure in the arms of a crude and sadistic lout, just as Huysmans' own ideal woman, Queen Marguérite of Navarre, prefers, among her lovers, a cook, a lackey, and a coppersmith. The Decadent element is omnipresent and foreshadows a later period of literary development. Again, throughout, love is equated with sado-masochistic perversity.

The total impression afforded by the prose poems is one of monotonous sameness. The briefer pieces are quick delineations upon a scene; the longer pieces, more extended elaborations. There are many flashes of an authentic variety of Decadent beauty. Unfortunately, too, there are occasional phrases that are unbelievably hackneyed, as in "Chlorotic Ballad": "Softly, draped in a hood of gray clouds, the twilight unfolded its misty tapestries over the melting purple of a setting sun." [3] This sort of diction quickly wears upon the reader's sensitivities.

Soon, in the full bloom of his Naturalism, Huysmans will drop such forced phraseology. Later, in his Decadent period, he will modify radically, and elaborate upon, this stylized manner, to the immediate enhancement of his reputation and the guarantee of his fame as a *décadent*. In the meanwhile, as evidenced by *A Dish of Spices*, his writing, as a whole, is far too poetic, far too brimming with intricate and involuted images, to be very satisfactory, or even, for that matter, to be tolerable reading for lengthy intervals. If Huysmans had stopped here, or if he had continued in the same guise, he would have become another pitiable failure in a minor genre.

II   Marthe

The first truly Naturalistic novel of Huysmans was entitled *Marthe, histoire d'une fille* (translated simply as *Marthe* in most editions), published by Gay at Brussels in 1876.

It is the disheartening, if not to say disgusting, story of an impoverished young girl, who aspires to become an actress, but who, instead, becomes a prostitute after a series of unfortunate love affairs and other assorted mishaps and tragic events. The heroine, Marthe, in typical Naturalistic manner, has no chance whatsoever of realizing her potentialities, such as they may be, or of succeeding in life. Her father, Sébastien Landousé, died of tuberculosis when she was only a child; her mother, Florence Herbier, when she was fifteen. So it is that Marthe, now orphaned, becomes, like her mother, a pearl blower, in an exhausting and most unhealthy trade, at a mere pittance of four francs per day. Her life is hell. Hence, from utter desperation, she becomes the mistress of a young man at her boarding house, almost without love or even the barest semblance thereof, just to forget the wretchedness of her work. At any rate, she does not last long under these sweatshop conditions. A sudden illness forces her to leave the factory.

In the most lurid Naturalistic manner, one personal tragedy follows another in a concatenation of events. She is, for instance, abandoned by her first lover. Then she begins to live with another man, whom she meets by chance at a cheap dance hall in the Rue du Cherche-Midi. Her griefs are soon compounded. She becomes pregnant by still another man, as she confesses to her second lover, and even bears the illegitimate child, one freezing night in December, during which her newborn infant dies of exposure and her new lover, unnamed, from a severe attack of dropsy. She is shaken in her inmost being. Thus she turns to alcohol for consolation, and shortly thereafter, with no other means of livelihood, becomes a prostitute. She plies her new trade, however, only for a short interval.

Marthe sinks more deeply into grief and despair. She is at the point of total collapse when Ginginet, a theater director by profession, chances into a small café on the Boulevard Saint-Michel one night, and, so to speak, discovers her. Only a fortnight later, as a fledgling actress, she makes her début on the legitimate stage at Bobino's. There, feverish with excitement, she revels in her new life; and there she forgets the wretchedness of her former existence.

At this time, Leo, the writer, the drama critic, enters the scene. He is, of course, the mouthpiece of Huysmans, who describes him in the following paragraph:

He lived by his pen; that is to say, he lived by starving. Torturing his ideas and endeavoring to set down the extravagances that haunted him, he had found himself with snapping nerves, and an immense fatigue had crushed him. From time to time, in his good moments, he would write a page swarming with terrible grotesques, with succubi and larvae in the manner of Goya, but the next day he would be incapable of getting out four lines, and he would end by painting, after extraordinary efforts, portraits which were beyond the bounds of all criticism.[4]

Their love affair is, by turns, fierce, tender, painful, lachrymose, saccharine. Bobino's theater goes bankrupt, however, in a sudden turn of events; and Leo loses his job upon the failure of the journal for which he works. Marthe and Leo commiserate with each other. They take solace in each other's arms for their common misfortune. It is in this context that Leo welcomes Marthe, his unemployed mistress, into his drab apartment. Here they quickly grow tired of each other and engage in frequent arguments. Their love, or rather their passion, is rapidly burning itself out.

The fire of their mutual suffering, nonetheless, burns all the more brightly. Leo's mother falls suddenly and critically ill. When he rushes to her side, Marthe takes advantage of his absence to visit her old friend Maria. It is she who warns Marthe that the police are still pursuing her because of her former activities in prostitution. She is terrified, understandably, upon learning of the pursuit, and starts to drown herself in the Seine. But Ginginet happens upon the scene and forcibly restrains her from committing suicide. Shortly thereafter, Marthe is apprehended by the police. The very next morning, Ginginet takes a sadistic delight in notifying Leo of her arrest. Leo is doubly grief-stricken, of course, but continues to care for his mother another week before returning to Paris.

Marthe feels deserted. Hence she seeks refuge in the house of Titine, her friend, a former actress at Bobino's. While there, she meets and attracts an elderly man, who undertakes to support her in a large apartment of extravagantly wretched taste. She flexes her sagging curves amidst her transient opulence.

Soon, however, Marthe tires of the importunities of her elderly lover and even of her life of ease. So it is that, most unexpectedly, without invitation, she returns to Leo's home. He is, of course, astonished to see her. It is an awkward meeting of singular embarrassment. For he has taken a new mistress, and certainly he no longer loves Marthe. Their rupture, as Huysmans observes drily, seems final and complete:

He gazed at her, astonished with himself because he no longer felt any desire for this woman, whom he once had kissed so ardently. He no longer felt anything but shame, a sort of sinking feeling, at having submitted to caresses which she, undoubtedly, distributed so generously to all whom she met in the course of business.[5]

Needless to explain, Leo rejects her summarily.

The events of the dénouement, in typical Naturalistic fashion, are somewhat anti-climactic. Ginginet degenerates into an impoverished and diseased guttersnipe, who dies of penury and alcoholism in the Hôpital de Lariboisière. A prematurely aging Marthe returns dejectedly to the brothel where she used to live and work. Leo marries a simple little drudge and evolves into the very caricature of a "bon bourgeois." So, in these ways, the character development of a theater director, of a writer, and of a beautiful young actress is ironically completed in their common ruin.

On such a pessimistic, almost nihilistic, note ends a novel which, though relatively weak and immature, enjoyed a modest *succès de scandale* in its day. As a treatment of the familiar Naturalistic theme of prostitution, its faults are immediately apparent, and were apparent even to the less sophisticated and more cursory readers of its own time. Indeed, the plot structure is crude, the characterization one-dimensional, and the style frequently rough and awkward. The total impression left upon the reader, even at the relatively uncritical time of publication, when the subject of prostitution had some shock value, is one of sketchiness and incompletion.

Nevertheless, there are certain felicitous paragraphs, which almost invariably foreshadow the style and structure of Huysmans' later Decadent period. In retrospect, these Decadent motifs and elements seem to comprise the part of the novel which has best survived. The Naturalistic elements of the novel either fatigue or amuse, by turns, in their unending chain of death, doom, damnation, and despair, in which nothing fortunate ever happens to anyone. What seemed daring in the late nineteenth-century, the study of vice and prostitution, is today of little interest in iself. Thus, whereas the novel did cause ripples of curiosity and interest upon publication in its own day, *Marthe* has not survived well and seems less satisfactory now than ever before. Astute critics of its own time considered the work, for the most part, as a literary disappointment of some merit and promise. Today *Marthe* seems, quite baldly, just a disappointment.

III   Les Soeurs Vatard

Les Soeurs Vatard (*The Vatard Sisters*), which was never translated, was published by Charpentier at Paris in 1879.

The novel opens, at once, upon a Naturalistic world of profanity and bestial sexuality, amidst the grimy factories and filthy bars of the slums of Paris. Within this depressing framework the two female protagonists, Désirée and Céline, slave away as common workers in the House of Débonnaire. Huysmans depicts the physical traits and characteristics of the two sisters in the following manner:

Désirée, une galopine de quinze ans, une brunette aux grands yeux affaiblis, pas très droits, grasse sans excès, devenante et propre, et Céline, la godailleuse, une grande fille aux yeux clairs et aux cheveux couleur de paille, une solide gaillarde dont le sang fourmillait et dansait dans les veines, une grande mâtine qui avait couru aux hommes, dès les premiers frissons de sa puberté.[6]

(Désirée, a fifteen year old urchin, a brunette with great weak eyes, rather askance, not too plump, comely and well-scrubbed, and Céline, the bar-fly, a tall girl with bright eyes and straw-colored hair, a strapping young wench whose blood coursed hotly through her veins, a great bitch-hound who had run after men from the very first intimations of puberty.)

The two sisters are straight from the gutter. Their determined quest of men, their desperate and rather pathetic search for love and affection, provide, almost alone, for their brief interludes of happiness, détente, or explosive relaxation, from their workaday world of drudgery.

So it is that, for her part, Désirée immediately and self-consciously falls in love with Auguste, a handsome young worker who has just been employed by the Débonnaire Company. She is smitten, so to speak, by his blond mustaches. Still, for some time, in a kind of shy playfulness, they simply remain close friends and inseparable companions. Then, finally, inevitably, their affectionate impulses deepen into a moment of passion.

Thus Auguste enters the life of the family. Against Céline he feels a momentary irritation, which passes in time. He shares their little transient joys, which are almost pitiable in their penury; and he joins into their familial quarrels and difficulties. But when a newcomer, Cyprien Tibaille, enters upon the scene, Auguste increasingly feels ill at ease. He even begins to drift away from Désirée and her family.

For Cyprien Tibaille is an esthete and a painter. It is he who seduces Céline. She does not understand him, of course, nor does he expect her to. Yet their lack of communication, of basic sympathies, creates most of their difficulty. Nevertheless, she loves him, perhaps not always wisely, or even well, but always with a saccharine and an often lachrymose display of affection. Cyprien Tibaille responds to her as an artist, whom Huysmans depicts in the following terms:

C'était d'ailleurs un homme dépravé, amoureux de toutes les nuances du vice, pourvu qu'elles fussent compliquées et subtitles.[7]

(He was, moreover, a depraved man, in love with all the possibilities of vice, provided they were complex and subtle.)

and

Il ne comprenait, en fait d'art, que le moderne. Se souciant peu de la défroque des époques vieillies, il affirmait qu'un peintre ne devait rendre que ce qu'il pouvait fréquenter et voir; or, comme il ne fréquentait et ne voyait guère que des filles, il ne tentait de peindre que des filles.[8]

(He understood, as far as art was concerned, only the modern. Caring little for the discarded effects of earlier periods, he maintained that a painter should put down only what he could touch and see; now, since he scarcely saw or came into contact with anything more than loose women, he tried, then, only to paint women.)

In this matter, it must be added, he entertains grandiose projects. Still, he achieves no success with his paintings. The Salon refuses to exhibit them, and the public at large rejects them on the open market. This critical and popular assessment of his work only stiffens his pride and makes him more than ever difficult for a woman like Céline to understand, accept, and love.

A twin thread runs through the novel.

Auguste and Désirée suffer, too, in the grand tawdriness which is so characteristic of the Naturalistic style. The difficulties of young love are compounded with his pressing need for financial security. For Auguste entertains the thought of marrying her, without really desiring it, simply because he wishes to protect himself, through her aid in the many political stratagems necessary to maintain his job at the Débonnaire Company. Désirée is willing, even eager. But Père Vatard is unalterably opposed to the match because of Auguste's extreme poverty. His adamant refusal to permit the match, of course, only maddens Désirée with a consuming determination to marry Auguste.

Céline, for her part, undergoes her own share of agony. In the meanwhile, Anatole, her first lover of sorts, has disappeared; and Cyprien Tibaille has grown more difficult with each passing day. Père Vatard throws up his hands in despair over the general situation, and exclaims with horror:

J'ai deux filles; il y en a une qui ne veut épouser légitimement personne, et elle est encore plus insupportable que l'autre qui voudrait se marier et qui ne le peut pas. C'est vraiment décourageant, je ne sais quoi faire.[9]

(I have two daughters; one of them doesn't want to marry anybody legally, and she's by far a bigger strain than the other one, who'd like to get married but who can't. It's really discouraging; I don't know what to do.)

Père Vatard, needless to say, is shocked by the amorous and thoroughly immoral vicissitudes of his two daughters. He is hurt thoroughly as Céline and Auguste vacillate constantly in their relationship with each other. He is nonplussed as Désirée cools perceptibly toward Cyprien Tibaille. Indeed, the remainder of the book records little more than the incessant seesaw of emotion and emotionalism of Père Vatard's two daughters.

Nevertheless, as in Zola's works, all the personal motifs of character incident and delineation remain somewhat minor. They return to, and are subsumed within, the larger motifs of the Naturalistic work-day world. Hence, in the dénouement as in the beginning, Céline and Désirée are, once more, primarily envisioned as workers rather than as women of flesh and blood, of motivation, decision, and indecision. So it is that the foreman can say of them, in résumé, that marriageable girls are always a bother, and that once they do marry, they cease to be of any value at all. After the observation, which represents the sweatshop's evaluation of humanity, the two young women, the sisters, disappear, with their lovers, their family, under the anonymous grime, dirt, and smoke of the Naturalistic world.

Les Soeurs Vatard is another Naturalistic novel. It is easy to perceive what values its own time placed upon it: the working-class milieu; the so-called real world; men and women of flesh and blood, of nerves and human sympathies; of perspiration, toil, and animal relaxation. Thus *Les Soeurs Vatard*, as the depiction of such a world, was something of an innovation to an age of readers used to Romanticism and the exoticism of escape literature or to spectators habituated to to the *pièce à thèse*. It had novelty. It afforded a thrill in that sense.

Today, however, to a generation accustomed to the crassest realism, *Les Soeurs Vatard* has no novelty, and it does not afford a thrill. It is, at best, tedious reading. The subject matter seems inconsequential; the protagonists, both male and female, unexciting and uninspiring. One could only try to look at the novel with the discernment of one of the astuter readers of its own time. Even then, one is forced to conclude that the primary value of the novel is its rôle in the esthetic development of Huysmans. It is not even a cardinal work in the Naturalist movement.

IV   Sac au dos (Knapsack)

Huysmans wrote two versions of *Sac au dos*. He published the first version in *L'Artiste* at Bruxelles in 1877. It appeared, upon scrutiny, a much cruder work than the later and more polished version. However, there were few actual changes. "Pardon," for instance, was the name of the friend in the original version, whereas it was later modified to that of "Francis Émont." Moreover, this later version, published in *Les Soirées de Médan* in 1880, was much better organized and more like a contemporary story. Otherwise, Huysmans did not significantly alter the original form.

In *Sac au dos*, of course, Huysmans portrays himself, in some depth, and describes his adventures while he is a conscript in the French army. As such, it is not a tale of flashing arms and victorious battles. It is the story, rather, of another pitiably untrained young Frenchman, suddenly inducted into the Sixth Battalion of the Garde Mobile, and rushed to the front in a futile effort to stem the onrushing Prussian tide. It is the account of the hero's rather unheroic bout with ennui, with exhaustion, and with chronic dysentery. It is the vivid recital of his dreary days spent in the company of the wounded and the syphilitic at the army hospital, and of their unexpected and forced evacuation to Châlons. It is the ordeal of their stifling and crowded trip, by train, to Arras. There ensue their days of suffering. There, too, the hero, or, rather, the anti-hero, if that is indeed the correct appellation, is consoled by Sister Angèle, an angel of mercy, who assuages his pain and affliction. And there, finally, he learns of Napoléon III's surrender at Sedan. Then, ill, lonely, and heartsick, he returns home from the Great Débâle to a beleaguered city.

It is at once apparent that *Sac au dos* is a very intimate work, which Huysmans composed from a painfully considered recollection of his war-time adventures. He was rather youthful when he composed the novel. Thus he did not have much breadth of experiences from which he could draw.

The novel is brief, perhaps overly brief; and the total impression given by its structure is one of sketchiness. There are few characters in the work, and except for the unnamed Huysmans himself, none has much depth. It is a record of the hero's impressions of war and its ravaging effects upon the minor personages with whom he comes into contact during its duration. The prose style is spare; the plot structure, slight. The action moves rapidly along episodic lines. It culminates very quickly in a dénouement of despondency and despair set from the first lines of the initial chapter.

Altogether, *Sac au dos* is one of Huysmans' better youthful efforts. It is almost unique by dint of having few or no Decadent overtones. Its prose is easy, natural, graceful, at least in the second version. Its economy makes the novel a masterpiece of this kind of memoir.

V   Croquis parisiens (Parisian Sketches)

Croquis parisiens, which was published by Vaton at Paris in 1880, is, as a collection of prose poems, something of an interlude in Huysmans' Naturalistic period.

Nevertheless, there is still a certain Naturalistic atmosphere which permeates the entire work, particularly the section entitled "Types de Paris." These prose poems carry titles like "Le Conducteur d'omnibus," "L'Ambulante," "La Blanchisseuse," "Le Geindre," and "Le Coiffeur." "Le Marchand de marrons," for instance, is typical with its evocations of a small chestnut shop, with its flaming oven, with its pathetic cuckolded proprietor and his coquettish wife.

Huysmans evidences his Naturalism, further, with the section entitled "Paysages." There he depicts the meandering filth of a river, scarcely more than a stream at times, called "La Bièvre." There, too, in a story of the same name, he etches a memorable picture of La Rue de la Chine; and in another story, with the identical title of the subject, he peoples le Cabaret des Peupliers with its unforgettable and diverse types. Then, in a prose still highly steeped in Naturalistic phrases and rhythms, he describes the "Vue des remparts du Nord-Paris."

Such episodic structure and such Naturalistic structure are present in certain other prose poems from other sections of the volume. "Le Poème en prose des viandes cuites au four" and "Un café" are noteworthy examples. In "Le Gousset" Huysmans achieves the effect of a Naturalistic *tour de force* by writing the following lines:

The Naturalist

Il est des odeurs suspectes, équivoques comme un appel dans une rue noire. Certains quartiers du Paris laborieux les dégagent lorsqu'on s'approche, l'été, d'un groupe. L'incurie, la fatigue des bras qui ont peiné sur d'accablants travaux expliquent l'âpre fumet de bouc qui s'élève des manches.[10]

(There are suspicious odors, as equivocal as a call in a dark street. Certain workers' quarters of Paris exude them when one approaches, in summer time, a group of people. The carelessness, the exhaustion of arms which have labored over crushing work explain the acrid billygoat smell which arises from the armpits.)

There has rarely been such an indelible, and repulsive, evocation of smell. Huysmans further evidences his Naturalistic descriptive powers in "Les Folies-Bergère en 1879" and "Le Bal de la Brasserie européenne à Grenelle."

There are also certain elements of an Impressionistic Decadence in *Croquis parisiens.* The sections entitled "Natures mortes" and "Paraphrases" are evidence of this current in the prose poems. Of special interest, along these lines, are "Cauchemar," "L'Ouverture de *Tannhäuser*," and "L'Image d'Épinal." "Le Hareng" is particularly colorful and scintillates with a Decadent style:

O miroitant et terne enfumé, quand je contemple ta cotte de mailles, je pense aux tableaux de Rembrandt, je revois ses têtes superbes, ses chairs ensoleillées, ses scintillements de bijoux sur le velours noir, je revois ses jets de lumière dans la nuit, ses traînées de poudre d'or dans l'ombre, ses éclosions de soleils sous les noirs arceaux.[11]

(O glistening and lusterless smoked herring, when I contemplate your coat of mail, I think of the paintings of Rembrandt, I see his superb heads once more, his ruddy flesh colors, the glistening of his jewels upon black velvet, I see again his jets of light in the night, his trails of golden powder in the shadows, his blossoms of suns under black arches.)

And in "Cauchemar" the reader sees already foreshadowed the "putrescent" style and even the exotic subject matter that will later characterize *A Rebours:*

Telles les visions évoquées dans un album dédié à la gloire de Goya, par Odilon Redon, le Prince des mystérieux rêves, le Paysagiste des eaux souterraines et des déserts bouleversés de lave; par Odilon Redon, l'Oculiste Comprachio de la face humaine, le subtil Lithographe de la Douleur, le Nécroman du crayon, égaré pour le plaisir de quelques aristocrates de l'art, dans le milieu démocratique du Paris moderne.[12]

(Like visions evoked in an album dedicated to the glory of Goya, by Odilon Redon, the Prince of mysterious dreams, the Landscape painter of subterranean waters and of deserts topsy-turvy with lava; by Odilon Redon, the Comprachio-Oculist of the human face, the subtle Lithographer of Suffering, the Necromancer of the pencil, misplaced for the pleasure of some aristocrats of art, in the democratic setting of modern Paris.)

Yet such purple prose is rather atypical of *Croquis parisiens* as a whole. It becomes a notable characteristic only during a later period of his literary development, i.e., in the full flowering of his Decadent style.

It is immediately evident that *Croquis parisiens* was not a major work. Obviously, too, such an ambitious aim was far from Huysman's design. The author simply attempted, with a young man's penchant for the prose poem, to depict the strange yet ordinary beauty of the workaday world of Paris. And while that beauty was in the main Naturalistic, it was nonetheless germane with—or infected with, as some would say—certain Decadent elements.

VI En Ménage (Housekeeping)

En Ménage was published by Charpentier at Paris in 1881.

In this novel, once again, Huysmans depicts himself, or at least certain aspects of his basic character, under another name. Once more, too, he displays a brilliant Naturalistic style, though one colored by uncommon nouns, exotic diction, peculiar rhythms, archaic structures, strange juxtapositions, self-conscious discords and dissonances. In short, he runs through, or rather performs, all the stylistic possibilities available to the Naturalistic prosemaster.

As Émile Zola observes somewhat reprovingly to his pupil, there is not much plot to the novel. The intrigue is baldly simple in a kind of presentation of a slice of life. One night, upon returning home, a husband finds his wife in another man's arms, upon his own bed, in the very act of adultery. He is too painfully outraged and too deeply hurt to react actively to the scene. He sim-

ply leaves home, crestfallen and overwhelmed, and resumes a dis-
ordered kind of bachelor's life. Rather unfeelingly he has relations
with several mistresses, one after the other. Then, one night, when
his wife comes to him, throws herself upon her knees, and im-
plores his forgiveness, they become reconciled in a lachrymose
flood of joy. Yet, very soon, they begin to tire of each other and to
irritate each other, as Huysmans says, in the eternal suffering and
the eternal stupidity of life.

There are, of course, greater depths to the book, particularly in
the direction of psychological analysis. Hence the relationship of
the two male protagonists, André and Cyprien, is particularly interesting. For it is to his friend Cyprien that André turns desperately, when he leaves his wife in disgust after seeing her con-
torted in pleasure in the very act of adultery. Cyprien is
thoroughly uninterested in this instance and evidences only an
esthetic bachelor's shrug at his friend's conjugal plight. His philosophy, in brief, is incarnated in the following lines:

Il haïssait d'ailleurs la bourgeoisie dont la corruption endimanchée
l'horripilait; il n'avait d'indulgence que pour les filles qu'il déclarait
plus franches dans leur vice, moins prétentieuses dans leur bêtise.[13]

(Moreover, he hated the bourgeoisie whose well-dressed corruption
made his flesh crawl; he was tolerant only to strumpets, who, he
stated, were more candid in their vice, less pretentious in their stupidity.)

André, for his part, expresses his philosophy in another passage:

—C'est égal, il y a des gens bien heureux. A table ou au lit, ils obtien-
nent, en guise de fourniture et de réjouissance, en plus de ce qui leur
est dû, un peu d'illusion! Nous, rien du tout. Nous sommes les mal-
heureux qui allons éternellement chercher au dehors une part mesurée
de fricot dans un bol; Au fond, ce n'est pas réjouissant ce que je dis
là.[14]

(—It's all the same, they are very happy people. At table or in bed,
they obtain, in the way of supplies and rejoicing, a little illusion, in
addition to what is owed them! We, for our parts, nothing at all. We
are the unfortunate ones who are going to look eternally, outside, for

a measured dish of stew in a bowl! Basically, what I say there isn't heartening.)

The two men invariably proclaim a cavalier philosophy of and attitude toward life. Ironically, however, they are, at heart, only *bons bourgeois*, particularly André. And it is as aristocrats *manqués* that they suffer drearily in the actual tedium of diurnal existence.

So it is that this little tragedy of marriage, adultery, and middle-class life opens in the hearth of the Désableau family. It is with Papa and Mama Désableau, who are childless, that Berthe Vigeois, their niece, is living. There life passes for her, as for them, in the drudgery of little things. It is there, too, that her young suitor, André Sayant, a writer, intrudes. And there, after a suitable time of courtship, despite Papa Désableau's disapproval of the literary profession, young André asks for, and obtains, her hand in marriage.

Very rapidly their marriage becomes, in a word, hell. Invariably Berthe is irritated with André, whom she henpecks upon every possible occasion. They have constant domestic troubles and frequent disputes. Rupture seems omnipresent. At length, it is Cyprien Tibaille, the painter, who, as Andre's closest friend, tries to reconcile them. But he wins only transient successes, while their conjugal war continues unabated. Perhaps he is an exemplary arbiter of art, indeed, but certainly not of domestic felicity.

The inherent problem of the marriage is apparent. Berthe, as Huysmans portrays her, is a reflection in a minor key of the prototype of Mme Bovary. So it is that she incarnates all the bourgeois pettiness as she reflects upon the husband whom she married without love:

Plus elle y pensait, plus elle était à présent convaincue qu'elle avait commis une sottise en l'épousant. Après avoir manqué des mariages avantageux, elle aurait dû attendre encore. Parmi les gens empressés autour d'elle dans les rares salons où son oncle acceptait de la mener, elle aurait pu découvrir un prétendant plus mondain, plus riche. Dans tous les cas, ces gens-là avaient des positions honorables, pouvaient, en travaillant, augmenter leur avoir, rendre l'existence de leur femme plus large. André s'occupait de littérature, une position méprisée par toutes les familles qu'elle connaissait, une position qui consistait à tourner ses pouces et à écrire la valeur de deux lettres par jour. Du reste, il ne pouvait avoir du talent, puisque le peu de livres qu'il avait écrits ne se vendaient point.[15]

(The more she thought of it, the more she was now convinced that she had made a blunder by marrying him. After failing to materialize one of several possibilities of a good marriage, she should have still waited. Among the people in a hurry around her in the few salons where her uncle consented to lead her, she could have discovered a richer suitor with a higher station. In any case, these people had honorable positions, and could, by working, increase their income, and make their wives' situation more comfortable. André was interested in literature, a profession looked down upon by all the families which she knew, a profession which consisted in twiddling one's thumbs and in writing the equivalent of two letters per day. Besides, he couldn't have any talent, since the few books which he had written did not sell.)

Berthe, too, yearns for the demanding arms of an ideal lover. She yearns for a kind of crass masculinity which her husband does not have. And she is vocal with this criticism, as with other points, to her friends, as they unsheathe their claws.

Berthe discovers this lover, or thinks she does, anyway, in Alexis. Yet her pleasure in adultery is small, as, again, Mme Bovary discovers, too, for her part. And Alexis, after being caught in bed with her, refuses to marry her. He is adamant, to Berthe's chagrin. He claims that he is impoverished and that the divorce would be a scandal. In short, he rejects her and abandons her with post-haste determination. Berthe, for her part, falls into a nervous crisis.

Yet, once free of his unfaithful wife, André is still not happy. His maid Mélanie does not fill the vacuum created by Berthe's absence. The weeks of separation pass. Rapidly his first days of tranquillity and release pass into the dullness of tedium. His wife fades into a sad and attenuated memory. He becomes, once again, the bachelor that he was before his marriage. Once more, too, he turns to his old friend Cyprien for the sympathetic understanding of his friendship.

So it is that André degenerates. He is given to rêveries. He indulges in erotic fantasies of women whom he once possessed in time past. He begins to frequent a harlot, more from the ache of loneliness than from the impetus of lust. In this frame of mind, he runs across Jeanne, his old mistress. With faint interest André resumes their relationship of five years before. But their relationship leaves him basically unsatisfied:

Le renouveau de leurs amours étant épuisé, André et Jeanne n'eurent bientôt plus que de béates tendresses, de maternelles satisfactions à coucher quelquefois ensemble, à s'allonger simplement pour être l'un près de l'autre pour causer avant de se camper dos à dos et de dormir.[16]

(The renewal of their loves being exhausted, André and Jeanne soon had no more than complacent caresses, maternal satisfactions, in sleeping together upon occasion, in stretching out simply to be close to each other, in order to chat before turning over, back to back, and falling asleep.)

Such a liaison is doomed from its inception, of course, and soon André terminates it. Once more he finds himself alone and wretched.

Finally, through the intervention of the Désableau family, André is reconciled to Berthe. Yet his return to bourgeois quietude and its concomitant satisfactions, all in a minor key, represents his total defeat, i.e., his final and irrevocable acceptance of the world as it is. For immediately André begins to be miserable with Mélie. In the meanwhile, Cyprien marries Mélie; and each friend despises the other's wife. In this light, it is Cyprien who terminates the novel with his melancholy observation:

—C'est égal, dis donc, c'est cela qui dégotte toutes les morales connues. Bien qu'elles bifurquent, les deux routes conduisent au même rond-point. Au fond, le concubinage et le mariage se valent puisqu'ils nous ont, l'un et l'autre, débarrassés des préoccupations artistiques et des tristesses charnelles. Plus de talent et de la santé, quel rêve! [17]

(It's all the same, don't you think, what surpasses all known morals. Although they branch off, the two roads lead to the same point of rendezvous. Basically, liaison and marriage have the same value since they have freed both of us from esthetic concerns and carnal longings. No more talent, but rather health, what a dream!)

And so the novel ends, with sudden finality, upon this note of bourgeois despair.

As in the dénouement, *En Ménage* is throughout an extremely pessimistic novel. Huysmans seethes quietly but steadily with a kind of bourgeois disillusionment. His spleen, his debilitating consciousness of the *taedium vitae*, are written on every page. His moody and introspective temperament sometimes flares into irascibility. His chronic melancholia becomes acute upon occasion.

En Ménage, however, is not a great novel, like Flaubert's work on a similar theme, *L'Éducation sentimentale*. It is too much the novel of one-dimensional characterization, i.e., once again of Huysmans' projection of his own personality into that of his characters. It is too much a lackadaisical account of adultery and casual liaison in a minor key. It is too much the recital of the trivia of life without a deep investigation of the meaning of those trivia.

Yet, at the same time, *En Ménage* is a good novel. Huysmans strikes and maintains a note of excellence in his mastery of the Naturalistic style. His pervading atmosphere of bourgeois despair is compelling. His portrayal of the spirit of his times is just and moving. His compassion for his pitiable creatures, caught as they are in inexorable circumstance, is always evident. His novel, in other words, catches the imagination, directs it along the lines of its double plot structure, and impels the reader forward. In this sense, it is a satisfying novel. While not a masterpiece of the Naturalist period, while not one of Huysmans' most enduring works, *En Ménage* remains today, nonetheless, an eminently readable and enjoyable novel. It is not dated, though it proceeds from a period as specific as that of French Naturalism. It lives.

VII A Vau-l'Eau (Down Stream)

A Vau-l'Eau (*Down Stream*), which was published by Kistemaeckers at Brussels in 1882, is Huysmans' masterpiece of Naturalistic pessimism and, perhaps, one of the best works of its type of the entire Naturalistic period.

It is the story of a young man, Jean Folantin, twenty-two, who comes from a poor family. After taking his baccalaureate, he becomes an employee in a ministerial office at a salary of fifteen hundred francs. He is a sensitive young man, an esthete, who is rapidly disillusioned with pretty women of his acquaintanceship no less than by his dull and uninspiring work at the Ministry. So it is, in this defeatist frame of mind, that, succumbing to spleen, he begins to drift, so to speak, down-stream. For Folantin's ennui is so terrible that, having no passion, he yearns for one: sexual gratification, professional advancement, gambling, anything at all.

Thus *A Vau-l'Eau* is a supreme example of the French cerebral novel of the late nineteenth-century. Decadence, abulia, and hypochondria abound in Jean Folantin's impressions and reactions to those sense impressions. Indeed, the novel is, for the most part, the record of sensations. Of particular interest, for example, are his sharp impressions of the book stalls along the Seine. One of his finest pleasures is to wander along the stalls, stop, browse, and rummage through old books and prints. He is obsessed with cuisine and the culinary arts. Every second day he visits, and devotes hours to, the baths. He takes an esthetic interest only in religious matters. Upon the death of a favorite cousin, Sister Ursule-Aurélie Bougeard, he reflects how life flows by relentlessly in its splendid monotony. Although he has no real faith, still the religious way of life appeals to him for its order and harmony.

Consequently the book is almost like a series of short stories. One of them records an evening passed at a small restaurant in the company of M. Martinet, an acquaintance: the fatigue; the boredom; the solitude; the reminiscences and memories; the mechanical mastication; the tasteless food; in the end, the crushing loneliness of it all.

Life, for Jean Folantin, is a great deception. It is emptiness. It is the taste of ashes in his mouth. It is the relentless unfolding of frustration and disappointment. In the dénouement, for instance, he is intensely disappointed by his relations with a woman, who offers herself to him in a small restaurant, and whom he later takes to his apartment in an unsatisfactory evening of somewhat perfunctory stimulation and response. The final scene concludes on the following note:

While reasoning in this manner, he had arrived at his house. Wait a minute, I have no matches, he remembered, digging into his pockets on the stairs. He entered his room, a breath of cold air froze his face, and as he walked forward in the darkness, he sighed: The simplest thing is to go back once more to the old pot-house, to go back tomorrow to that frightful sheep-pen. But what's the difference? There's no doubt of it: The best does not exist for fellows without a sou; only the worst ever happens.[18]

Defeat, here in the conclusion, as on the first page, is the omnipresent theme.

Thus *Down Stream,* though brief, is the apogee of Huysmans' Naturalistic period. Never has a Naturalist hero, or, rather, anti-hero, been more a combination of cerebral decadent and utterly abject bourgeois at the same time. In this singularly depressing novel, Folantin is the supreme example of a dejected hero. In the sense that he is something of a cerebral decadent, he foreshadows Des Esseintes of *A Rebours.* But he is also more. For more than in any of his other heroes, Huysmans is incarnated in Folantin. For this analysis of the essential character of Huysmans, then, *Down Stream* is both noteworthy and memorable. The novel is, perhaps, Huysmans' most satisfying of his Naturalist period.

CHAPTER 3

The Decadent

PERHAPS Huysmans works into his so-called Decadent period, after his interest in Naturalism wanes, through his studies in art criticism.

I   L'Art moderne

L'Art moderne, a collection of essays on contemporary art, was first published by Charpentier in May, 1883. At once, it encountered a dual reception. Traditionalists and formalist critics decried what they considered to be Huysmans' excesses and his over-emphasis on Impressionism. However, several of the more perspicacious critics, like Geffroy, Bourget, and Mallarmé, praised the book enthusiastically.

In *L'Art moderne* Huysmans is concerned with contemporary painting during the years 1879 through 1882. He writes about the Salon of 1879, the Exposition of the Independents in 1880, the Official Salons of 1880 and 1881, and the Exposition of the Independents in 1881. The Appendix concerns his observations on art in 1882. In these essays Huysmans extolled the contributions of the Impressionist painters above all. He analyzed Cézanne with compassion and understanding. He professed his admiration for the greatest of the Decadent painters, Gustave Moreau. He exhausted superlatives whenever he wrote of Degas. He ranged the whole of contemporary painting, in short, and except for Moreau, he made judgments which are still considered valid, on the whole, today. Huysmans, like Baudelaire before him, was, indeed, the most singularly discerning art critic of his generation.

II   A Rebours

The Decadent period proper begins for Huysmans in the following year.

The Decadent

A Rebours (*Against the Grain*) was published by Charpentier at Paris in 1884. From the outset the novel has been recognized as the masterpiece of the late nineteenth-century French Decadent literature. Moreover, its protagonist, Duke Jean des Esseintes, has become the very prototype of the Decadent hero.

There is almost no plot, or intrigue, to the novel. It is, rather, the record of an esthetic young aristocrat's response to, and sensations about, the world. Des Esseintes is interested in little more than sensual experiences and gratifications. For him the world is no more than a vast exotic garden from which he may pluck, according to his fancy, the various blooms of his perverse delights.

Duke Jean des Esseintes has a peculiar childhood. As a school boy, he is not very good in any subject other than Latin, and he evidences no interest or inclination for anything else. He is an isolated, melancholy child. As the years pass, he becomes more and more of a misanthropist; and his nerves, ever raw, become increasingly tender. His young manhood is the record of a sometimes titillating and an always debilitating debauchery. Finally, he tires of that. Even in his twenties, as Huysmans writes, "one passion and one only, woman, might have arrested him in this universal disdain that was rising within him; but this too was exhausted." [1] Still, jaded beyond utterance, Des Esseintes wallows through year after year of excess in Paris. Thus it is that, in Huysmans' words, he ends his second decade of riotous living:

Sole surviving descendent of this family, once so numerous that it covered nearly all the domains of the Ile-de-France, and of La Brie, was the Duc Jean des Esseintes, a frail young man of thirty, anaemic and nervous, with hollow cheeks, eyes of a cold, steely blue, a small but still straight nose, and long, slender hands. [2]

He feels that Paris is unhealthful for him, that it has no more to offer. He turns from the city in disgust.

Des Esseintes visualizes a salubrious life in the country, as well as the new mode of existence which it would undoubtedly bring to him:

He determined to sell the Château de Lourps, which he never visited and where he would leave behind him no tender memories, no fond regrets; by this means he paid off all claims on the rest of property, bought Government annuities and so secured himself an annual income of fifty thousand francs, while reserving, over and above, a round sum to buy and furnish the little house where he proposed to steep himself in a peace and quiet that should last his lifetime.[3]

After selling the ancestral manor, Des Esseintes takes with him only his two old servants, husband and wife, to his ideal cottage at Fontenay-aux-Roses.

There he redecorates his monastic retreat. He paints his walls in exotic colors, he relishes the designs of fine rugs, and he caresses his expensive *objets d'art*. He relaxes in a peculiar library filled primarily with Latin authors of the decadence. He blends subtle shades of liqueurs and experiments daily with a large array of perfumes. He even sketches misty and ephemeral pictures in the air with his perfume atomizer. He relishes reproductions of Moreau and Goya. He drinks in deeply the odors of the exotic plants that grow luxuriantly around him. He even has a tortoise beautifully inlaid with jewels, so that it creates a sparkling pattern as it slowly moves, stones glittering, across the deep rugs of subdued colors. Huysmans describes it in the following passage:

Once back from the jeweller's who had taken it in to board at his workshop, the beast blazed like a sun in splendour, throwing its flashing rays over the carpet, whose tones were weak and cold in comparison, looking for all the world like a Visigothic targe inlaid with shining scales, the handiwork of some Barbaric craftsman.[4]

Des Esseintes, in short, enjoys a Decadent esthete's paradise in his retreat.

Yet Des Esseintes also lives a Spartan life in his double existence. His typical régime is something like this:

At five o'clock in winter, after dusk had closed in, he ate an abstemious breakfast of two boiled eggs, toast and tea; then came dinner at eleven; he used to drink coffee, sometimes tea or wine, during the night, and finally played with a bit of supper about five in the morning, before turning in.[5]

He delights in the self-denial of this kind of monastic isolation. Indeed, he has turned to Fontenay-aux-Roses primarily to escape the noise and bustle of Paris:

Worst of all, he loathed with all his powers of hate the new types of self-made men, the hideous boors who feel themselves bound to talk loud and laugh uproariously in restaurants and cafés, who elbow you, without apology, on the pavements, who, without a word of polite excuse or so much as a bow drive the wheels of a child's go-cart between your legs.[6]

Des Esseintes, alone in his study, is much given to introspection. He indulges himself in memories and sexual reveries, which debilitate him with their stark intensity:

As a matter of fact, he issued from these reveries utterly exhausted, half dying; then he would at once kindle the candles and lamps, flooding the room with light, thinking in this way to hear less distinctly than in the darkness the dull, persistent, intolerable beating of the arteries that throbbed and throbbed unceasingly under the skin of the neck.[7]

It is a nightmarish existence. At such times he relives the past while experiencing the identical reaction that he had to the original event. He recalls the street boy, Auguste Langlois, whom he once corrupted and tried to make into a murderer. He recollects Miss Urania, the American acrobat with the lithe and masculine body. He ruminates over the possibility of traveling, especially to England and to Holland, his two favorite nations.

Des Esseintes begins to experience a nervous crisis. He is incapacitated to the point of insomnia, dyspepsia, and a muscular collapse. He poses but cannot resolve certain philosophical questions which obsess him. Chief among them is the fundamental problem of decadence. He thinks repeatedly, obsessively, along these lines:

Yes, nobility was utterly decayed, dead; aristocracy had fallen into idiocy or filthy pleasures! It was perishing in the degeneracy of its members, whose faculties grew more abased with each succeeding generation till they ended with the instincts of gorillas quickened in the pates of grooms and jockeys, or else, like the once famous houses of Choiseul-Praslin, Polignac, Chevreuse, wallowed in the mud of legal actions that brought them down to the same level of baseness as the other classes.[8]

He knows that, like his epoch, he, too, is decadent. Yet the new men, the new decadents, he ruminates, are even more corrupt and rotten than he is:

More nefarious, more vile than the nobility it had plundered and the clergy that it had overthrown, the bourgeoisie borrowed their frivolous love of show, their decrepit boastfulness, which it vulgarized by its lack of good manners, stole their defects which it aggravated into hypocritical vices. Obstinate and sly, base and cowardly, it shot down ruthlessly its eternal and inevitable dupe, the populace, which it had itself unmuzzled and set on to spring at the throat of the old castes.[9]

It is to escape this new, and more debased, brand of decadence that Des Esseintes has fled for refuge to Fontenay.

Yet, ultimately, there is no refuge in his artificial world of Fontenay. Des Esseintes plumbs and exhausts the range of human possibility in his vain effort to reactivate his lethargic body and to awaken his dormant senses. He surrenders. He ceases to work upon his body, whipping it on, stimulating it like a homo-duplex, one part of his psyche watching the other half act and react. Now he sinks, rather, into deep lethargy. His senses fail to react any longer, his spirit can endure no more, and he suffers a complete physical collapse. The village physician, who goes to him at his urgent plea for attention, warns the young man against the dangers inherent in such luxurious living. Des Esseintes, at his end in Fontenay, his ideal pleasure house, must return to Paris, to health, and to sanity. Still, the decadent hesitates:

Des Esseintes dropped into a chair, in despair: "In two days more I shall be in Paris," he exclaimed; "well, all is over; like a flowing tide, the waves of human mediocrity rise to the heavens and they will engulf my last refuge; I am opening the sluice-gates myself, in spite of myself. Ah; but my courage fails me, and my heart is sick within me!—Lord, take pity on the Christian who doubts, on the sceptic who would fain believe, on the galley-slave of life who puts out to sea alone, in the darkness of night, beneath a firmament illumined no longer by the consoling beacon-fires of the ancient hope.[10]

So it is that Des Esseintes remains, to the end, both unsatisfied and insatiable.

III *Evaluation*

Several observations may be immediately made about the novel.

First, the character of Des Esseintes himself is ever the focus of interest for this masterful study of Decadent psychology. He is the very quintessence of the late Romantic, or Decadent. In him Huysmans paints a memorable, and, very probably, an immortal portrait of the effete esthete whom even depravity has ceased to titillate. Hence *A Rebours* is the scintillating record of the sentiments and sensations of the Decadent hero rather than an example of the traditional plot or intrigue. Its very lack of plot structure sets it apart from the mainstream in the traditional development of the French novel. *A Rebours*, then, from the structural as well as from the stylistic standpoint, is not only different; it is also, and more importantly, unique as a French novel. It is a contribution in kind as well as one of depth.

Second, and as an observation related to and proceeding from the first point, *A Rebours* is an esthetic innovation and an outstanding *tour de force* which, more than any other novel of the period, incarnates the ideas and values of French literary Decadence. Its style is involuted with its various and varying decadences. Its imagery glows with the many colors of a magnificent mosaic. Its vocabulary is a veritable repository of exoticisms. Certain scenes, in particular, shine with a preternatural brilliance. Its structure is elaborate, throughout, and perhaps overly elaborate in many if not in most of the somewhat disconnected passages which, together, form the body of this singular novel. From the viewpoint of form, therefore, *A Rebours* is the richest treasure-house of Decadent esthetics, from which, indeed, the principles of Decadent philosophy may be extracted.

Third, the novel is charged, and even surcharged, with an electric emotionalism at once shattering and indelible. After the experience of such a book, Huysmans had indeed but a single choice: the butt of the pistol or the foot of the Cross. That he chose the latter, despite the latent anticlericalism of his Naturalistic years, is ample testimony of the magnitude of his crushing despair. It is significant that Dorian Gray, in Oscar Wilde's novel of that name, read and admired *A Rebours*. For that novel had an immediate and resounding success which continued throughout the Decadent period proper and well into the twentieth century. It is, once read, an unforgettable novel. Its place is secure as Huysmans'

finest work and as one of the authentic masterpieces of the nineteenth century and, indeed, of the whole of French literature.

IV   En Rade (At Harbor)

En Rade, which was published by Tress and Stock in Paris on
April 26, 1887, was in its way, something of an interlude in the
development of Huysmans' Decadent period.

There is, to be sure, something of an equivocal quality to the
book, clearly discernible from certain of its more decadent attri-
butes. Yet Huysman's Naturalism is also apparent, and immediately so, from both his gruesome descriptions and his sensitive
portrayal of rural psychology. These same Naturalistic techniques,
however, are frequently turned back upon themselves in the
novel. Consequently they, too, tend to function *à rebours,* i.e.,
against the grain. Moreover, through the three dream sequences
inserted into the novel, Huysmans, once more, has recourse to familiar Decadent motifs which he had already enunciated in *A Rebours.* For example, one paragraph reads:

Dans leurs démences hermétiques les songes avaient-ils un sens? Arté-
midore avail-il raison lorsqu'il soutenait que le Rêve est une fiction de
l'âme, signifiant un bien ou un mal, et le vieux Porphyre voyait-il juste,
quand il attribuait les éléments du songe à un génie qui nous aver-
tissait, pendant le sommeil, des embûches que la vie réveillée pré-
pare? [11]

(In their hermetic madness did the dreams have a meaning? Was
Artemidorus right when he maintained that the dream is a wisp of
imagination of the soul, signifying a good omen or an evil omen, and
did old Porphyrus see correctly when he attributed the elements of
dreaming to a spirit which warned us, during sleep, of the pitfalls
which awakened life prepares?)

Again, in another passage, which reveals the involutions of Decadent prose, Huysmans writes:

Plusieurs nuits se succédèrent, des nuits où l'âme élargie de sa misé-
rable geôle voleta dans des catacombes enfumées du rêve. Les cauche-
mars de Jacques étaient patibulaires et désolants et laissaient, dès le
réveil, une funèbre impression qui stimulait la mélancolie des pensées

déjà lasses de se ressasser, à l'état de veille, dans le milieu de ce château vide. Aucun souvenir précis de ces excursions, dans les domaines
de l'épouvante, mais un vague rappel d'événements douleureux tra-
versés par d'alarmantes conjectures.[12]

(Several nights followed, nights during which the enlarged soul of his
wretched jail fluttered in the smoking catacombs of the dream. Jacques'
nightmares were as frightening as the gallows, and just as grieving, and
left, from his awakening on, a funereal impression which stimulated
the melancholy of thoughts already tired of resifting itself, in the
waking state, in the midst of this empty château. No precise memory
of these excursions, in the domains of terror, but a vague recall of
mournful events shattered by alarming conjectures.)

The examples might easily be compounded *ad infinitum*, but ex-
emplification for its own sake is pointless. So it thereby becomes
apparent, from these citations, that, in a sense at least, this novel,
too, through such Decadent elements, becomes something of an
inverted form of materialism. It is a small wonder, then, that the
novel remains somewhat unclassified and, indeed, unclassifiable.

The very plot structure of *En Rade* is baldly uncomplicated. In
this story, quite simply, Huysmans relates how Jacques Marles,
the protagonist, is forced to seek refuge from his numerous credi-
tors at Lourps, with Louise, his ailing wife. There he leads, or
rather endures, a singularly subdued existence in its own minor
key. Rapidly he surrenders himself to solitude, to passivity, to in-
dolence, to introspection. Again and again his mind turns in upon
itself, as he obsessively examines and re-examines his thought
processes. Increasingly he regards his life, his spouse, and the ever-
narrowing limits of his restricted world with hypochondriacal las-
situde. Even his departure from the château, in the dénouement,
cannot assuage his agonizing pain:

Cette idée qu'il allait enfin quitter Lourps, rentrer à Paris, retrouver
son intérieur, son cabinet de toilette, ses bibelots, ses livres, le trans-
porta; mais quoi? ce départ ferait-il taire la psalmodie de ses pensées
tristes et décanterait-il cette détresse d'âme dont il accusait la défection
de sa femme d'être la cause? [13]

(This idea that he was going to leave Lourps finally, to return to Paris,
to find his study again, his dressing room, his odds and ends, and his

books, delighted him. But what? would this departure cause the in-toning of his melancholy thoughts to be still, and would he slough off this soulful distress for which he blamed his wife's desertion as the cause?)

Such is the substance of the novel. And so it is that the life of Jacques Marles, especially during his forced retreat to Lourps, seems, for the most part, the prosaic saga of a strange and hitherto unencountered combination of Decadent and Naturalist spleen.

En Rade is difficult to evaluate.

As a novel, it is structurally the portrait of a soul-state of the Naturalist-Decadent protagonist Jacques Marles, and hence the evocation and, to a large extent, the picture of the evolution of the novelist himself, Joris-Karl Huysmans. Here, in this analysis of the fictional hero, and thereby in his own self-analysis, Huysmans achieves his most lasting effect. Otherwise, the novel leaves much to be desired. Indeed, it is even somewhat ineffective.

The style, for instance, is rather undistinguished. It is neither Decadent nor Naturalistic, and it cannot be classified as repre-sentative of either of Huysmans' great periods. In this novel Huysmans simply has his moments, stylistically speaking, but does not sustain a great flow of diction and imagery.

The characterization, in particular, is not noteworthy. Huysmans understands Jacques Marles, to be sure, for it is of himself that he writes in this personage. Otherwise, however, the men and women are stodgy, they are wooden, and they do not really live. They lack the substance of life and the compelling motivations of passion, love, hatred, jealousy, or any other consuming emotion.

From the philosophical standpoint, the novel is far from a ma-jor achievement. Indeed, it is a novel of a minor key, but it does not even ring the minor key in a memorable way. In it Huysmans is not a Catholic writer, as he later is; or a Decadent writer, as most assuredly he can be, and perhaps most effectively at that; or even a Naturalistic writer, as he was, and with brilliance, in *Down Stream*. The book leaves the reader unsatisfied, uncertain, and with a tepid flavor in his mouth.

Thus *En Rade*, perhaps, among his so-called major endeavors, is Huysmans' greatest disappointment.

V   Un Dilemme

Un Dilemme was published in Paris by Tresse and Stock in 1887. Like several other works by Huysmans during this period, the novel is singularly difficult to classify.

Indeed, *Un Dilemme* is not even a novel. It is, rather, a *nouvelle*. As such, it recounts the story of a notary, Maître Le Ponsart, and of his obdurate son-in-law, M. Lambois, and of their reactions to a very delicate family situation at Beauchamp, a little village in the Marne. It seems, as the plot develops, that M. Lambois has worked for many years to get his son, Jules, named as sub-prefect. He is finally at the point of success. However, the sudden death of his son destroys his tantalizing dream, and his hope for the future darkens further when his personal fortune is endangered. Thus with much bitterness, now, he wants to enter the Conseil Général, with the guidance and support of M. Le Ponsart.

Hence the intrigue of the novel reveals itself as baldly simple. The structure of the *nouvelle* turns upon the fact that Mlle Sophie Mouveau appeals to M. Le Ponsart that his son-in-law, M. Lambois can and should help her, but will not do so, although she is illegitimately pregnant by his deceased son, Jules. Indeed, M. Lambois has dismissed her summarily. Thus Sophie Mouveau goes away, defeated, overwhelmed, and dies in abortive childbirth. Her acquaintance, if not her only friend, the Widow Champagne, writes M. Le Ponsart to entreat him for the little money necessary for a proper burial. He refuses. M. Le Ponsart snorts to himself that it has been a waste of the three sous postage for her even to make such an idiotic request. In a dénouement which recalls some of the most horrible moments of truth of Naturalistic literature, M. Le Ponsart observes to himself:

Cependant il faut avouer que notre bienveillance, pour son souvenir, est peut-être entachée d'égoïsme, car enfin, si nous n'avons plus rien à craindre de cette fille, qui sait si, au cas où elle eût vécu, elle n'aurait pas de nouveau jeté le grappin sur un fils de famille ou semé la zizanie dans un ménage.[14]

(Yet one must admit that our benevolence, for its memory, is perhaps tainted by egotism, for at length, if we no longer have anything to fear from this girl, who knows whether, in case she had lived, she wouldn't have again thrown her hooks upon some family or sown discord in some home.)

It is difficult, even in Naturalism, to go beyond this point of crassness.

Thus, just from the account of the plot structure, *Un Dilemme* is immediately recognized to be a Naturalistic piece of writing. The intrigue, such as it is, turns upon an old Naturalistic theme. The details are Naturalistic. The descriptions are Naturalistic. The characterizations are naturally conceived and executed. Yet an element of Decadence makes itself apparent from time to time. The reader must look for the so-called Decadent elements of this *nouvelle*, but the point is that he can find certain instances of involuted style or, at least, of a style richer and more complex than the Naturalistic style. Then, too, there is something of a Decadent philosophy that permeates the flavor of the *nouvelle* and some of the characterizations. Consider the case of M. Le Ponsart, for instance. A widower at sixty-five, he is something of a rustic philosopher, and by no means a Naturalistic boor or lout or a super-annuated peasant or squire interested only in money. In the following lines the "decadent" element is present in the *nouvelle* as much as it can be, i.e., in something of the personality of M. Le Ponsart and also in Huysmans' choice of words to depict him:

Puis il eut ce retour philosophique sur la vie qui succède si souvent à la première torpeur des gens dont l'esprit se met à ruminer, quand l'estomac est joyeux et le ventre plein. C'est égal, ce que les femmes s'entendent à gruger les hommes! se disait-il, et il se complaisait dans cette pensée sans imprévu. Peu à peu, elle se ramifia, s'embranchant sur chacune de ses qualités corporelles qui contribuent à investir la femme de son inéluctable puissance. Il songeait au festin de la croupe, au dessert de la bouche, aux entremets des seins, se repaissait de ces détails imaginaires qui finirent par se rapprocher, se fondre en un tout, en la femme même, érotiquement nue, dont l'ensemble lui suscita cette autre réflexion aussi peu inédite que la première dont elle n'était d'ailleurs que l'inutile corollaire: Les plus malins y sont prise.[15]

(Then he had this philosophical twist upon life, which so often follows the first torpor of people whose minds begin to ruminate when their stomachs are satisfied and their bellies full. What difference does it make that women are skilled in swallowing up men! he told himself, and he took pleasure in this unexpected thought. Little by little, it divided, branching out on each of its corporeal qualities, which help invest woman with its ineluctable power. He daydreamed about the banquet of the thighs, the dessert of the mouth, the side-dishes of the breasts; he feasted upon these imaginary details, which finally drew together, melted together, into the same woman, excitingly naked, whose general view caused him to have a thought just as little unanticipated as the first, of which it was, moreover, only the useless corollary: The most cunning are trapped there.)

Certainly these lines do not afford the substance of Decadent literature proper. The flashing images, the scintillating turns, the exotic words are not there. On the other hand, such writing differs from Huysmans' own prose during his more, or most, Naturalistic moments, in the full bloom of his first and Naturalistic period. Moreover, such writing differs in tone and quality from that of the other Naturalists. The exemplifying paragraph in question, to be sure, is not truly Decadent, by any means. But by no means, either, is it typically Naturalistic. It seems, rather, to swerve away from the Naturalistic and towards the Decadent, as if moving from one pole to another like the swinging of a pendulum.

What, then, is the value of *Un Dilemme*?

First, it should be remembered that the work is a *nouvelle,* not a novel. Hence, and the second point to be stressed, the characterization cannot be extensively developed, or perhaps even sufficiently developed. The protagonists are sketches of men and women, not full-bodied portraits. Third, the plot structure, or, rephrased, the interrelationship of men and women, is quite thin, simply for lack of space necessary to a fuller and more comprehensive development. Fourth, it must ever be kept in mind that the *nouvelle* is a "tight" genre in literature. The plot structure must be manipulated within very constricting limits. Hence any *nouvelle* tends to be valuable primarily from the standpoints of prose style and of characterization. This particular *nouvelle* is no exception.

What conclusions may be drawn?

From the standpoint of style, *Un Dilemme* is neither markedly Naturalistic or Decadent. Indeed, the prose is rather undistinguished, too. There are few scintillating images or choice metaphors. There is an almost total absence of involution or exotic diction. But from the standpoint of characterization, *Un Dilemme* can be remembered, with much pleasure, for some of the deft sketches of its men and women. The example of M. Le Ponsart comes to mind. He is brilliantly portrayed as a prototype of the crafty old squire, ruminating upon money and women in that order. It is a full-bodied and even lusty portrait of a man, which could well come from the brush of a Flemish master. In such characterization lies the true value of *Un Dilemme* and its warranted claim to permanency as a *nouvelle* in French literature.

VI   Certains (Critical Papers)

Certains was published at Paris by Tresse and Stock in 1889. It is an interesting collection of essays, notes, analyses, and interpretations on diverse aspects of the subject of art. In this sense, very largely, the work is a completion of *L'Art moderne*.

In this book, again, Huysmans reveals his esthetic penchant and his critical acumen. Once again, too, he reveals himself as an uncannily perceptive, and receptive, art critic, within the "decadent lineage," for lack of another term. His very choice of subject matter, for instance, is indicative. He is concerned with the idea of dilettantism, with eroticism in painting, and with the appearance of monsters in painting throughout the evolving centuries, and particularly with the appearance of monsters, grotesques, and gargoyles during the Middle Ages. Not only are many of his topics of discussion, evaluation, and elaboration "decadent," then, but also, and more importantly, his "treatment" thereof, or mode of approach thereto, is markedly Decadent in both style and perception. Thus *Certains*, a volume of art criticism, is one of the terminal works of Huysmans' so-called Decadent period.

Huysmans also shows himself as something of a philosopher in this book. He is not so much a philosopher in an academic or traditional sense, of course, as an urbane commentator on matters of life and art. His "decadent" worldview evidences itself within this context.

In one of these *Critical Papers*, as the title exists in the English translation, Huysmans writes upon the subject of dilettantism. Indeed, that is the very name of the essay, "Of Dilettantism." In it, too, the word "dilettantism" resumes the pejorative connotation which it had before the advent of the dandy. During the period of dandyism, it will be remembered, dilettantism became something of an article of faith in the gentleman's credo. Such a concept is no longer the case with Huysmans. Dilettantism, for him, is merely superficiality and prosaic misunderstanding. Hence, in this essay, Huysmans attacks the "bon bourgeois" for his superficiality, for his bad taste, for his many clichés, for his prosaic misunderstanding of art and its function. Huysmans demands seriousness of tone and treatment. Yet dilettantism of the most degenerate sort is the rule of the day. So it is, he observes, that utterly frivolous conversation pieces provide the substance of most popularist and reputations. He concludes:

Happily, this profitable state in which the dilettante finds himself has another side. His excesses of pusillanimity, his debauches of prudence are fatal, and his language, becoming weak and driveling, returns to the dull and leaden style of the Institutes or liquefies in the humid verbalisms of M. Renan. For there can be no power, if one does not love with passion or hate with passion. Enthusiasm and scorn are indispensable in creating a work of art. Power is to the sincere and the ill-tempered, not to the indifferent and the skulking.[16]

Huysmans takes his stand for emotion, indeed, but also for cogency in emotion. He always observes the distinction.

In *Critical Papers,* as he wanders from topic to topic, Huysmans always reveals his critical acumen. He is a paragon of taste. He champions great painters before they become popular. He is not in the least afraid to take a stand and to defend his position. For instance, in his essay entitled with the painter's name, Huysmans makes one of his many famous prophecies:

I am not a prophet, but if I am to judge by the ineptitude of the enlightened classes, who, after having for long condemned Delacroix, do not yet suspect that Baudelaire is the poet of genius of the nineteenth century, that he towers a hundred feet above all the others, including Hugo, and that the masterpiece of the modern novel is the *Education sentimental* of Gustave Flaubert,—and yet, literature is said to be the one art that is most accessible to the masses!—if I am to judge by this, I can believe that this truth, which I am the only one to write today, concerning M. Degas, will probably not be recognized until after an unlimited period of years.[17]

This glimpse into the future, like nearly all of Huysmans' predictions, came true in its time. From these lines, too, it is evident that Huysmans' choices and predilections presage the taste of the better art critics of the succeeding generation. Indeed, along with Baudelaire, Huysmans may be said to be one of the two great French writers of the nineteenth century who possess a supremely good faculty for judging art and painting.

At the same time, and in the same essays on Degas, Huysmans shows further evidence of his discursive interest in philosophy and philosophical matters. In this instance, he discusses the notion of Degas' misogny, in general while subordinating it to the broader concept of a particular painting:

But in addition to this special note of hatred and contempt, the most visible thing in these works is the unforgettable veracity of types, depicted with a thoroughly and ample draughtmanship and with a lucid and masterly passion, as though the whole had been done in a cold fever. The thing to be seen is the dull yet ardent color, the mysterious and opulent tone of these pictures, the supreme beauty of flesh, rendered bluish on rose-red, by the water and lighted by closed windows, draped in muslin, in sombre rooms, in which, by the veiled daylight of a court, are to be discerned walls hung in Jouy cretonnes, washstands and tubs, flasks and combs, wooden-backed brushes and footwarmers in rose-copper.[18]

It is apparent from this passage that Huysmans is by no means the critic of the generalized concept. He subordinates theory, always, to the practical considerations of color, design, brush work. He grounds his esthetics in the most practical matters of painting and, hence, of artistic evaluation. Herein lies much of his enduring contribution to art criticism.

Huysmans, as might be expected, is quite interested in so-called "decadent painting." Of this type, of course, the supreme and uncontested master is Gustave Moreau. It is natural, then, that Huysmans should pen an essay, by that name, upon this painter. In one paragraph of assessment, Huysmans, as revealed here, shows himself almost as involuted in his style as the Decadent subject matter about which he writes:

One identical impression surged up from these various scenes, an impression of spiritual onanism, repeatedly but chastely performed; the

impression of a virgin with a body of solemn grace and a soul exhausted by the reflections of solitude, by secret thoughts; the impression of a woman, self-retained, yet raving and crying out, in the
solemn formulas of dark prayers, invitations to sacrilege and to lust,
to torture and to murder.[19]

Huysmans evidences his interest in Moreau not only in this essay,
but also, of course, through Des Esseintes in *A Rebours,* and in
certain other references in various works. It is interesting to note
that, almost alone of all the painters whom Huysmans was among
the first to champion, Gustave Moreau has failed to maintain the
niche claimed for him.

Huysmans reveals his interest in "decadent art" in "Félicien
Rops" also. In this essay he makes a detailed study of several of
Rops's paintings. Of course, he is drawn to Rops through the
painter's interest in satanism and the religious motif and in his
elaborate and profuse usage of erotic designs. Of the occult element in Rops, Huysmans writes:

He has, in a word, celebrated that spirituality of Lust which is Satanism; he has painted, in imperceptible pages, the supernatural side of
perversity, that heaven-and-hell which lies beyond all Evil.[20]

As a matter of fact, Huysmans even tends to understand the eroticism in Rops's work within a broader and religious, or rather occult, context:

In art, this mental hysteria, or morose delectation, is forced to translate
itself into works which shall fix the images it has created. It finds there
its spiritual exhaust is, as I have said, the surest means of destroying
art.[21]

VII   La Bièvre

La Bièvre was published by Genonceaux at Paris in 1890.

It is strange that such a work should come precisely at this
point in Huysmans' life and development. Certainly it represents
something of an interlude during his Decadent period. It comes in
time after the great Decadent masterpiece, *A Rebours;* yet it ante-
dates Huysmans' other great Decadent novel, *Là-Bas.* Thus the

book is a kind of suspension of momentum during this stage of the author's literary and intellectual evolution.

At first glance the book is simply the story of a river, La Bièvre, which traverses Paris. But it is also much more than that. The river is sometimes incarnated as a woman. She possesses a personality of her own. She develops. She changes. She undergoes varying and progressive soul-states. She lives.

Huysmans is concerned with, and paints, her changing moments of mood in her course. That is always his primary concern. Moreover, it is a philosophical concern, as evidenced by frequent musing and meandering reflection. It is a poetic concern, as illustrated by personification and simile. The following paragraphs, for instance, are typical of Huysmans' study of the river:

La Bièvre représente aujourd'hui le plus parfait symbole de la misère féminine exploitée par une grande ville.

Née dans l'étang de Saint-Quentin, près de Trappes, elle court, fluette, dans la vallée qui porte son nom, et mythologiquement, on se la figure, incarnée en une fillette à peine pubère, en une naïade toute petite, jouant encore à la poupée, sous des saules.

Comme bien des filles de la campagne, la Bièvre est, dès son arrivée à Paris, tombée dans l'affût industriel des racoleurs; spoliée de ses vêtements d'herbes et de ses parures d'arbres, elle a dû aussitôt se mettre à l'ouvrage et s'épuiser aux horribles tâches qu'on exigeait d'elle.[22]

(Today the Bièvre represents the most perfect symbol of feminine wretchedness exploited by a great city.

Rising from the pool of Saint Quentin, near Trappes, she flows, still slender, into the valley which bears her name, and mythologically incarnated, as one imagines her, as a scarcely pubescent girl, a wisp of a water-nymph, still playing with her doll, under willow trees.

Like many country wenches, the Bièvre fell into the industrial quarter of pimps upon her arrival in Paris; despoiled of her clothing of grass and her ornaments of trees, she must have gone to work immediately and wears herself out at the horrible tasks demanded of her.)

Such is the tone of the work. Such is its poetry.

Perhaps the greatest value of *La Bièvre* lies in its place in time and space in the work of Huysmans. It offers a kind of relaxation in the relentless progression of his Decadent period towards *Là-Bas*. As such, it is at once a throw-back to his earlier and Naturalistic period, with its grimy descriptions, and a foreshadowing of his later and spiritualistic period, with its concern for the eternal matters of the human soul.

VIII   Là-Bas (Down There)

Là-Bas (*Down There*), which was published by Tresse and Stock at Paris in 1891, is the last of Huysmans' Decadent novels; and, as such, it terminates the so-called Decadent period of his life.

The work is also significant for certain pronouncements of the author's concept of the fundamental nature of Naturalism. For here, once more, in the foreword, he attacks the very principles of the Naturalist school to which he once adhered:

Ce que je reproche au naturalisme, ce n'est pas le lourd badigeon de son gros style. C'est l'immondice de ses idées . . . C'est d'avoir incarné le matérialisme dans la littérature . . . C'est d'avoir glorifié la démocratie de l'art. Quel miteux et étroit système! [23]

(What I reproach naturalism for is not the heavy wash of its awkward style. It is the rubbish of its ideas. . . . It is having incarnated materialism in literature. . . . It is having glorified the democracy of art. What a shabby and narrow system!)

Certainly, with its curious subject matter, its twisting complexities, and its many involutions, *Là-Bas* is much more in the line of Gothicism than of Naturalism, and an erotic and thoroughly putrescent Gothicism at that.

Indeed, this constant preoccupation with the ideas of Realism, Naturalism, and Decadence is reflected in the novel itself. There are numerous philosophical discussions of the point between Durtal and Des Hermies, the two chief protagonists. In one scene particularly, Des Hermies launches a relentless attack upon Realism. Durtal agrees with him on the whole, but nonetheless makes certain reservations:

Realism is just as repugnant to me as it is to you, but that is no reason for denying the unforgettable services that it has rendered to Litera-

ture; for indeed it is the realists who have rid us of the artificial pup-
pets of Romanticism and rescued letters from a pedantic idealism and
the futility of an old maid's imagination fevered by celibacy! In a word,
following Balzac, they have created visible and palpable living creatures and placed them in their suitable environment; they have helped
on the development of the language initiated by the romanticists; they
have known genuine laughter and have even at times been vouchsafed
the gift of tears,—in fact, they have not always been carried away by
this fanaticial passion for the mean and the sordid that you talk
about.[24]

In these cogent points, which he makes one by one, Durtal emphasizes the fact that Realism has seemingly exhausted its subject
matter and reached an inevitable *cul de sac*. So he wonders, now,
what other literary avenues of possibility and choice there may be.
He rejects the contemporary scene, for his part, and chooses a
subject from the Middle Ages, i.e., the sadistic Maréchal Gilles de
Rais, nicknamed Blue Beard, for want of a better choice. In this
sense, furthermore, Durtal verbalizes Huysmans' own inevitable
break, years before, with Naturalism:

At bottom, as des Hermies maintained, there had all along existed between him and the other realists such a divergence of ideas that no
stable agreement could long continue. You abominate your age, he
used to say, they adore it; and that's the end of it. It was fated that
one day you were bound to make your escape from this new American
domain of Art and seek a more breezy and less dead level region.[25]

Fortunately, however, the novel is much more than a mere treatise on different schools of literature.

IX *Evaluation*

The plot structure of *Là-Bas*, such as it is, proceeds on two
levels.

First, there is, quite simply, Durtal, the man who, as a person,
moves in and through Paris, and within its labyrinth of inordinately strange persons and their peculiarly strange ways. Among
these fabulous characters there is Des Hermies, a medical doctor
who rejects the gadgetry of modern science, and believes, rather,
in herbs, in folk medicines, in absolute good and evil, and even in

demonic possession. Among them, too, there is Mme Hyacinthe Chantelouve, the vampire woman, the *femme fatale*, who, under the fictitious name of Mme Maubel, writes to Durtal her interminable letters of admiration and love. Her husband, M. Chantelouve, is an accomplished but somewhat disreputable Catholic historian, who writes lengthily but without overmuch comprehension upon the more abstruse and delicate questions of the holy faith and its mysteries. There is, also, Louis Carhaix, an impoverished bell-ringer, wed to a reticent wife; and it is he who waxes philosophical to Durtal and Des Hermies, who visit him, on the meaning of the true music of the Holy Church, like that of the ritual ringing of the great church bells.

Second, all these characters, who act, react, and interact within the frame of this city of nineteenth-century mist and mystery, move within a permeating atmosphere of diabolism. In this connection Huysmans makes the following observation:

To think that the century of positivists and atheists has overset everything except only Satanism, which it has not been able to drive back one step! [26]

and again, through a favorite mouthpiece,

It is easy to understand why, said Carhaix. Satanism is either ignored or unknown; it was Father Ravignan, I think, who showed how it was the Devil's greatest feat to succeed in getting himself denied. [27]

Indeed, such are the persons whom Durtal encounters and frequents in his peregrinations through the modern Babylon of Paris. The novel terminates, finally, with Durtal and his friends in the Carhaix apartment, while the election for General Boulanger goes on outside. The symbolism of this juxtaposition of spiritual with temporal is self-evident. And so the novel ends upon a note of total disgust with the nineteenth century and its Realistic atmosphere and political and social concerns.

Down There is evidently a strange novel. It not only pivots upon a singular plot structure, but also, in so doing, utilizes a weird assortment of characters. There is a strong element of eroticism in addition to the exoticism which pervades the work. The very atmosphere is bathed in the supernatural. Thus the novel exercises a strong and immediate appeal to all who love mystery and mysticism.

The prose style of *Down There* is Decadent, i.e., involuted, rich, and labored. The images are filled with conceits, similes, and metaphors. The organization of the novel, with its two concurrent themes, is in itself peculiar. The action progresses erratically. Thus the novel is indeed Gothic.

Down There is not the very summation of Decadence, as *Against the Grain* is. It is not a great *tour de force*, like its predecessor in time. Durtal does not live forever in the memory, as Des Esseintes does. But *Down There,* nonetheless, is a powerful and important novel. Its characterization of individuals, rather than types, is memorable. Its prose scintillates. The plot structure carries the reader on. Its subject matter of diabolism, or mysticism, versus the mundane reality of the nineteenth century is worthy of interest. All in all, *Down There* remains with the reader, and very often disturbingly so.

CHAPTER 4

The Spiritual Writer

I En Route

*E*N Route was published by Tresse and Stock at Paris in 1895. This autobiographical novel begins a new and final period in the author's life and artistic expression. This is the spiritual period, in which Huysmans is almost exclusively occupied with spiritual problems, as reflected in his numerous autobiographical writings on the faith and by his several studies in hagiography. Of course, one could reasonably expect this period to be the logical culmination of his spiritual development after the stress, the agony, the sin of his Decadent period. As a matter of fact, Huysmans had nowhere to go, now, other than the foot of the Cross, after he had exhausted all the neurotic desires of his flesh and perhaps a twisted mind. The dénouement was inevitable. It was natural. It was inherently logical. So it is that, in turning to the Church, Huysmans had come, in time, to fulfil the famous prophecy of Barbey d'Aurevilly. For upon reading the monstrously involuted, sick, and evil *A Rebours,* Barbey had noted that after such a book the author would have to choose between the muzzle of a pistol or the foot of the Cross.

By the time of *En Route,* then, the chips were down. Huysmans faced that choice. He made it. He embraced the Catholic faith, again, and threw himself upon God's mercy at the foot of the Cross.

Huysmans describes himself in *En Route* through his protagonist, Durtal, who is the author's mouthpiece throughout the novel. At once it is apparent that this work is not truly a novel, but rather a lengthy autobiographical confession. Furthermore, the work contains very little plot structure as such, and it records almost no external action. *En Route* is, rather, a psychological novel, i.e., a work of internal action. In this sense, too, it is the account of Durtal's conversion, or rather of his re-acceptance of the Catholic faith.

At the beginning of the novel, Durtal, like Huysmans himself, is no longer the creature of his flesh and the victim of his pursuit of pleasure. He is morally depleted. The taste of wine has soured in his mouth, and his head has been dulled from too much song. The initial fact of the novel is the state of Durtal's physical exhaustion and spiritual crisis. Indeed, the novel proceeds relentlessly, logically, rigorously from Durtal's realization that he is a sinful man. This self-knowledge is the point of departure in his conversion, or re-acceptance of the Catholic faith.

What was the moment of time that Durtal would call, afterwards, his conversion? Of course, the circumstance was during his meditation, i.e., his profound communion with himself, in the Church of St. Sulpice. He found it impossible to analyze the experience, however, beyond the time and place. Durtal simply knew, as he said later, that, after so many unhappy years of disbelief, he suddenly believed again, and that, just as suddenly, he began to feel happy again.

There were three major reasons for Durtal's conversion. First, Durtal came from a very old and very pious family, which had contributed several members to the holy orders; and this familial influence always remained strong. Second, he suffered from a severe melancholia, and utter disgust with life, a deep sensation of spleen, aggravated by his isolation and his esthetic interests. Third, he had, from his earliest childhood, a passion for art; and he was always drawn, even during his atheism, to the Church on account of its art. With such a background and such a constitution Durtal's conversion was not only explicable but also inevitable.

There were other reasons, cultural factors, intellectual convictions and interests. Durtal was fascinated by the priesthood. He adored the atmosphere of the Middle Ages. During his period of complete doubt he still visited the great churches and cathedrals. He was personally attracted to the Trappist way of life. As a man of letters, he was intrigued by the art of hagiography. He felt that it was a lost branch of literature, so to speak, no less than wood carving or miniatures upon old missals. As a matter of fact, Durtal himself noted that this predilection for hagiography, this consuming interest in the lives of saints, like those of Saint Teresa and

Saint John of the Cross, seemed to develop quite naturally from his interest in satanism. So it was that these factors, too, brought such forces of heredity and constitution into play that Durtal had nowhere to go, indeed, but to the Church.

In the following lines Durtal reveals his esthetic orientation to life as a whole and to its religious aspect in particular:

Ah! the true proof of Catholicism was that art which it had founded, an art which has never been surpassed; in painting and sculpture the Early Masters, mystics in poetry and in prose, in music plain chant, in architecture the Romanesque and Gothic styles. And all this held together and blazed in one sheaf, on one and the same altar; all was reconciled in one unique cluster of thoughts: to revere, adore and serve the Dispenser, showing to Him reflected in the soul of His creature, as in a faithful mirror, the still immaculate treasure of His gifts.[1]

Thus Durtal's religion is immediately apparent as that of the artist. But while Durtal's interest is artistic, his struggles with his conscience are singularly prosaic. He had a moral battle, day by day, sometimes hour by hour, to resist the temptations of the flesh. He finds it difficult to concentrate; his mind wanders as he seeks to devote himself to prayer. Penance is especially difficult and painful. The beauty of Catholic art, at such moments of trial, is his mainstay and succor. He can always lose himself in adoration of a beautiful and intricately carved wooden crucifix or in the aural delight of the strange melody of plain chant.

It is difficult for Durtal to change his evil ways. His former habits cling to him like the Old Man of the Sea. He struggles with himself in a constant battle for spiritual development. Hence, for him, the first great encounter lies with his former pessimism. Huysmans notes that Durtal speaks of the Church in this respect:

Once I despised her, because I had a staff on which to lean when the great winds of weariness blew; I believed in my novels, I had my art. I have to come to recognize its absolute inadequacy, its complete incapacity to afford happiness. Then I understood that Pessimism was, at most, good to console those who had no real need of comfort; I understood that its theories, alluring when we are young, and rich, and well, become singularly weak and lamentably false, when age advances, when infirmities declare themselves, when all around is crumbling.[2]

[83]

Such esthetic pessimism, as it might be properly termed, is incongruous with the true spirit of Catholicism. Thus Huysmans self-consciously sheds himself of it.

Huysmans' new faith is self-conscious to the extent that, in time, he can analyze the nature of it. In the following lines, for instance, he ruminates over his personal relation to the holy faith:

How doubt the truth of dogmas, how deny the divine power of the Church, for she commands assent?

First she has her superhuman art and her mysticism, then she is most wonderful in the persistent folly of conquered heresies. All since the world began have had the flesh as their springboard. Logically and humanly speaking they should have triumphed, for they allowed man and woman to satisfy their passions, saying to themselves there was no sin in these, even sanctifying them as the Gnostics, rendering homage to God by the foulest uncleanness.[3]

One must take into account the profound change in Huysmans since he wrote of himself through his mouthpiece, as protagonist, in Des Esseintes. Surely it is a clean division in religious and moral orientation and in his way of life.

As his faith deepened by progressive degrees, Durtal became more and more interested in the monastic life. He thought constantly of the beatific isolation of the monastery. He yearned for this separation from diurnal life and its pleasant but frivolous pleasures and anxieties. He longed for the beneficent silence of the cloistered life, for there he could find the spiritual nourishment which his soul desperately needed. He desired the life of monastic food, meditation, prayer, solitude, self-denial. Above all, he wished to taste and to satiate himself with the inexhaustible joys of Catholic liturgy and plain chant.

Thus it was that before long, his spiritual advisor, Abbé Gévresin, counseled Durtal to find solace in La Trappe. Durtal was, of course, a docile student, for he no longer seemed to possess any directive will of his own. His conversion had shattered him. Yet to some extent, perhaps, his French heritage rebelled against mysticism and the cloistered life. At least, Durtal noted a kind of insurrection in his soul. It died, nonetheless, as quickly as it had been born. He embarked on a life which would evermore be the greatest part of him: the life of spiritual reflection in the retreat.

Durtal's first few days at La Trappe were far from satisfactory. He thought that he could never get used to the severe discipline which the monastery demanded of him. He was agonized to make his first confession since childhood. It was a long and singularly detailed confession which cost him unfathomable suffering.

In the monastery, too, Durtal engaged in long theological discussions. He sharpened his religious sense and his moral sensitivity through such disputation. His understanding deepened progressively. Huysmans records in this connection:

Durtal perceived very plainly and clearly for the first time the distinction, the separation of the soul from the body, and for the first time also, he was conscious of the phenomenon of a body, which had so tortured its companion by its needs and wants, to forget all its hatred in the common danger, and hinder her who resisted it, the habit of sinking.[4]

His sojourn in the monastery, then, was unforgettable. It left its indelible imprint upon his character. Father Etienne and Father Maximin were catalysts who brought out the finest points of his religious self-consciousness.

Still Durtal was not a monk or even an oblate. The day came when he had to leave the monastery, and of course that day represented, too, his return to the Babylon of the megalopolis of Paris. Huysmans analyzes Durtal's depression upon his return to his home:

And he repeated to himself that the most difficult thing would not be to master the emotions of his flesh, but indeed to live Christianly, to confess, to communicate at Paris, in a church. He never could get so far as to that, and he imagined discussions with the Abbé Gévresin, his gaining time, his refusal, foreseeing that their friendship would come to an end in these disputes.[5]

His fears along this line were not realized. He knotted his friendship with the Abbé more firmly than ever. His faith was stronger than ever.

Durtal continued to grow spiritually. He attributed such growth, in large part, to his time in the monastery. Of his retreat he said that, indeed, he lived twenty years in ten days. After tasting the delight of such an experience, Durtal thought:

Paris and Notre Dame de l'Atre have rejected me each in their turn like a waif, and here I am condemned to live apart, for I am still too much a man of letters to become a monk, and yet I am already too much a monk to remain among men of letters.[6]

Durtal changed his orientation radically on all literary matters. Never again could he be the sophisticated writer, the decadent, which he had formerly been. Never again, indeed, could he be a denizen of the city which he had formerly so deeply loved. Huysmans, in this connection, depicted Durtal's return to his once beloved city:

And he was seized with such an access of sadness, such an outburst of despair, that he thought of getting out at the first station, and returning to the monastery; and he had to shrug his shoulders, for his character was not patient enough nor his will firm enough, nor his body strong enough to support the terrible trials of a novitiate.[7]

The die was cast. Durtal was, henceforth, a new man. He was a Catholic. His life was transfigured.

II Evaluation

En Route is a complex work to assess. Indeed, since it is such an introspective novel, it cannot be properly evaluated at all from the standpoint of plot structure. It has little, or none. From the viewpoint of characterization, only Durtal stands out, for it is ever he who is the focus of attention. In this sense, however, he is a masterpiece of analysis and understanding, for Huysmans has recorded himself after much study and reflection. From the aspect of style En Route is not a Decadent work. It reflects the author's new sobriety.

In a word, En Route is profoundly a Catholic novel: an excellent one.

III   La Cathédrale

La Cathédrale was published by Stock at Paris in 1898.

The work represented many years of study and reflection for Huysmans. He had always been interested in medieval church architecture, even during his most Decadent period when he was without faith. He had wavered for a long while, trying to decide whether to choose Reims, Amiens, Beauvais, Rouen, Bourges, or another cathedral. It was not an easy choice for him. But, at length, he focused his energies upon the great Cathedral of Chartres. This work was his great labor of love for the glory of Catholic art and architecture.

Huysmans did not expect success from the book. He thought that it would be so intensely limited as to appeal only to the most church-minded few. He was wrong. *La Cathédrale* became, very quickly, the most popular of all his works. This was true despite its emphasis on medieval symbolism and its often pedantic and encyclopedic discussions of statues, stained glass windows, and Stations of the Cross.

Along with the minute description of the Cathedral of Chartres, there runs the theme of Durtal's growing religious sense. Still, even now, there is a struggle between his desire to remain a writer and his wish to become a monk. Huysmans records the conflict in the following words:

Je suis depuis trente ans dans l'administration et j'en ai cinquante. Je vais bientôt pouvoir me reposer. Pourquoi perdrais-je mes droits à une retraite prochaine? Il sera toujours temps, quant je l'aurai prise, de me faire moine. Encore faudrait-il toutefois avoir la vocation. Le bon Père, directeur de Solesmes, en serait alors le premier informé. Je lui ai écrit, pas plus tard qu'hier, pour protester contre la résolution qui m'est prêtée. Non, le moment d'entrer en religion n'est pas venue pour moi. Dois-je le dire? J'ai passé dans les cloîtres des heures infiniment douces; mais le régime est au-dessus de mes forces. Je devrais demander des permissions spéciales pour manger trois oeufs par jour, sinon, je mourrais d'inanition. Vaut-il pas mieux, en attendant la retraite, rester fonctionnaire et écrire des livres? [8]

(I've been in administration for thirty of my fifty years. Soon I'm going to be able to rest. Why should I give up my rights to an early retirement? When I have taken it, it will not be too late to become a monk. Even then however I would need to feel a calling towards it. The good Father, director of Solesmes, would be the first to be informed of it. I wrote him, no later than yesterday, to protest against the resolution which is ascribed to me. No, the moment to enter religion has not come for me. Must I say it? I have spent exceedingly pleasant hours in the cloisters; but the diet is above my strength. I would have to ask special permission to eat three eggs a day, otherwise I would die from starvation. Isn't it better, while awaiting retirement, to remain a civil servant and write books?)

This kind of soul-analysis characterizes *La Cathédrale*. Indeed, other than actual descriptions of the Cathedral and analyses of its art and architecture, the character of Durtal affords the sole matter of focus.

Thus it is immediately apparent that *La Cathédrale* is difficult to assess from a literary standpoint. First, it is not at all a novel, but rather an autobiography concerned with medieval art and architecture. Second, there is naturally little concern with plot structure and the other niceties of form associated with the concept of the novel. Third, the work is such a perfect guide to the Cathedral at Chartres that some critics have called it something of a Baedeker guide. Indeed, it does seem, at times, to leave the domain of literature as it is generally understood. Too, the work was actually sold to visitors at Chartres as a guide to the great Cathedral. But within these limits, and understood in this context, *La Cathédrale* is a masterpiece. It comprehends medieval art as few works ever have embraced it, and at the same time it continues the spiritual development of Durtal.

IV   La Bièvre et Saint-Séverin

La Bièvre et Saint-Séverin was published by Stock at Paris in 1898. This was, of course, a new edition of *La Bièvre*, which had been previously published. But it was the first appearance in print for *Le Quartier Saint-Séverin*, which formed half of the volume in question.

It is easy to understand how the Saint-Séverin district of Paris appealed to Huysmans. Vestiges of the Middle Ages lingered in its kind of triangle, with its intersections, with its irregular lines. Huysmans even found in the quarter the same type of population which had inhabited it centuries ago. The beggars were still there, with the prostitutes, with the workers, with the elderly men and women who lingered along the street corners. The very movement of the section was slow. It seemed to Huysmans that time had, in a way, remained still through the centuries. Therein lay the charm of the quarter, and therein consisted its great appeal to him. He was angered by each innovation that the nineteenth century brought to the quarter. He was saddened as the crumbling shops were replaced one by one. He longed to see the quarter preserved as it was: a true relic of the Middle Ages.

Huysmans was explicit in his desire to maintain the quarter. He wrote at length about the Carmelites and the nuns of Saint Clare. In them, and through them, he saw the formula for preserving the oldest and most unchanged section of Paris. He wrote to the point:

Le remède est là et non dans cette destruction du quartier qu'on nous annonce. D'ailleurs tout le monde sait fort bien qu'on n'amende pas par départements l'âme des scélérats et que la salubrité d'une ville n'est pas mieux assurée parce qu'on agrandit les rues aux dépens des maisons et qu'on substitue aux vieilles puanteurs des allées et des cours la moderne infection des fumées et des eaux vomies par les usines.[9]

(Such is the remedy, not this destruction of the quarter which they tell us about. Besides, everybody knows very well that one does not amend the souls of rascals simply by moving them around, and that the health of a city is not the better assured because streets are widened at the expense of houses and because for the fetid odors of alleys and court-yards is substituted the contemporary malady of smoke and steam vomited forth by the factories.)

This was Huysmans' prescription to the malady of contemporary living in the great city of Paris. He realized, of course, that the megalopolis would not accept his remedy. Yet it remained his moral obligation, even his religious duty, to make his recommendation.

Thus this work, too, is almost impossible to evaluate. It is certainly not a novel. It is not even an introspective confession or self-study, like so much of Huysmans' other writing. It is, quite simply, the account of the author's impressions of the quarter of Saint-

Séverin. As such, it is filled with many similes, metaphors, descriptive passages, and even patches of purple prose. There is a certain monotony to the work, even in its brilliant evocation of the spirit of the Middle Ages. The digressions are sometimes tiresome. The structure itself seems, at times, somewhat inorganic; i.e., it does not proceed logically from one section to the other. On the other hand, the work is interesting, and it does occupy a significant place in Huysmans' thought.

V   La Magie en Poitou; Gilles de Rais

The year 1899 saw the publication at Ligugé of *La Magie en Poitou; Gilles de Rais.*

This work in two parts contributed little to Huysmans' literary reputation. Moreover, it represented a kind of interlude in his development as a spiritual writer. To be sure, it continued his interest in magic, satanism, and the occult, as his treatise on wizardry in Poitou so amply showed. Furthermore, he resumed in *Gilles de Rais* the interest in that medieval diabolist, a general of Joan of Arc, which he had already evidenced so fully and so well in *Là-Bas.*

Perhaps the study of *Gilles de Rais* is not even up to the level of Durtal's obsessive preoccupation with the man in *Là-Bas.* From the literary standpoint only the style of the work is in question, since neither part of the work is "literature" as such. The style, then, is competent. It does not represent a throw-back to the Decadent period. It is not so involuted or "gamey." It continues the momentum of the spiritual period. It announces the full-bodied prose of the spiritual period to come in Huysmans' next several volumes.

VI   Les Gobelins

In 1901, at Paris, the Société de Propagation des Livres d'art published *La Bièvre; Les Gobelins; Saint-Séverin.*

Only the section of the book entitled *Les Gobelins* was new, for both of the other parts of the work, *La Bièvre* and *Le Quartier Saint-Séverin,* had been previously published. Huysmans' studies of the river La Bière, and of certain quarters of Paris were so popular that new editions were justified from time to time. In this work *Les Gobelins* represented the author's interest in the lower-class, manufacturing district of Paris, named from the manufacturer of Les Gobelins.

Huysmans' depiction of this district in *Les Gobelins* relied very heavily upon his former Naturalistic technique and prose style. Such dependence was natural. The subject lent itself to Naturalistic depiction, for the substance of the work was about the working-class quarter and its poor conditions which the Naturalists so loved to describe. Perhaps, at times, Huysmans went too far in his descriptions. Perhaps they were strained, forced, too "naturalistic." More likely, such an impression was due to the fact that the author had simply passed from one period, the Naturalist period, through another period, the Decadent one, into the final period of his life, the spiritual period: And Naturalistic subjects were now foreign to him. Hence, in a sense, despite certain interest, *Les Gobelins* was a failure.

VII Sainte Lydwine de Schiedam

Huysmans published *Sainte Lydwine de Schiedam* with Stock at Paris in 1901.

The work was his first formal study in hagiography, though he had been intensely interested in the subject for several years. The actual writing did not come easily. He had to labor over it:

La préparation de son livre lui donnait, disait-il, "du tintouin." Il ne pouvait guère compter que sur les Bollandistes pour le guider dans ses investigations, et leur latin du XVIe siècle le rebutait. Dépourvu d'imagination, it avait besoin, pour prendre son élan, d'un point d'appui dans la réalité des choses. Il se plaignait de manquer d'assises à cet égard. Comment décrire l'humble logis où la Sainte, putréfiée vivante, avait souffert le martyre? Il n'était véritablement exalté que par la peinture de ses plaies sanieuses et nauséabondes. Le vieux naturaliste assoupi en lui se réveillait et fourbissait son style pour dédier à la suppliciée ce que le jongleur de Notre-Dame peut offrir à la Vierge Marie: ce qu'il sait faire.[10]

(The preparation of his book gave him, he said, some trouble. He could count on nobody but the Bollandists to guide him in his investigations, and their sixteenth century Latin repelled him. His imagination exhausted, he needed to take his running jump from a point of departure in reality. He complained about a lack of fundamental facts in this respect. How could he describe the poor quarters where the Saint, actually decaying while still alive, had suffered martyrdom? He was truly exalted only through the portrayal of her sanious and foul-smelling sores. The old dormant naturalist in him awoke and polished up his style in order to dedicate to the tortured woman what the juggler of Our Lady could offer to the Virgin Mary: what he knows how to do.)

This hagiographical study was, though arduously composed, something of a culmination of his spiritual period. Certainly Huysmans was not the same after the experience of writing the book.

Sainte Lydwine de Schiedam was primarily a study in the spiritual mystery of suffering. It was more than the hagiographical analysis of a woman, Saint Lydwine, who had suffered more physical agony from a greater number of known and unknown maladies than possibly anyone else in all history. Huysmans was concerned with the eternal lesson of her physical suffering. In this respect he focused his attention on the law of solidarity in evil and the law of reversibility in good. By this he meant, according to Catholic doctrine, that everyone was, in a sense, responsible for the evil of his fellow man, and that everyone could, in a sense, attribute to his fellow man the virtues which he himself possessed. Of course, the idea was foreign to the soul of Protestantism; yet it was fundamental to a concept of suffering in Catholic thought. Rephrased, this idea was known in Catholic theology, as mystical substitution. The supreme example was Jesus Himself, the Son of God, who owed nothing, truly, but who gave everything. So, in an analogy, Saint Lydwine, who owed little, gave nearly everything of herself in a kind of expiation for the sins of others. Such was the basis of the agony borne by the saints and by those in contemplative orders. Such was the basis of the incredible and the ineffable suffering of Saint Lydwine, catalogued in nauseating detail in Huysmans' study.

Thus much of the subject matter of *Sainte Lydwine de Schiedam* is, for lack of another term, "naturalistic." Thus, too, much of the writing is somewhat Decadent or involuted. Still, Huysmans moves more deeply into his spiritual period proper. Still, the analysis of Saint Lydwine as a compelling portrait of a Christian soul in unbelievable agony, rings truer to the soul of Naturalism than any of Huysmans' protagonists from his Naturalist period. And, as for sheer "corruption," conceived in utterly Decadent terms of blood and pus, this hagiographical study is something of the *ultima thule*. In summary, *Sainte Lydwine de Schiedam* is by no means Huysmans' finest book, or even one of the best books of his spiritual period. The Durtal saga of self-confession and introspection far excels it in terms of literary quality. On the other hand, *Sainte Lydwine de Schiedam* cannot be ignored. It is a fine and notable effort. In it the lost art of hagiography flares up in a brilliant revival.

VIII   De Tout

De Tout was published by Stock at Paris in 1901.

The work, essentially, is a collection of essays, prose poems, and impressions, divided more or less without definite plan into three sections, plus an appendix. Some of the subjects have been treated in previous books. Several of the subjects are written about here for the first time. Throughout the book the quality of writing is rather uneven.

Huysmans reveals himself as the acute observer of man and his foibles throughout the work. In the following paragraph, taken from "Les Habitués du café," he writes:

L'attrait que le café exerce sur ce genre d'habitués s'explique, car il est composé de desseins en jeu, de besoin de lucre, de repos aviné, de joies bêtes. Mais en sus de ces habitués dont la psychologie est enfantine et dont la culture d'esprit est nulle, il en est d'autres sur lesquels l'influence despotique agit: des habitués riches ou de vie large, célibataires invaincus sans ménage à fuir, gens sobres exécrant le jeu, ne parlant point, lisant les journaux à peine. Ceux-là sont les amateurs désintéressés, les habitués qui aiment le café, en dehors de toute préoccupation, en dehors de tout profit, pour lui-même.[11]

(The appeal exercised by the café upon this kind of customer is easily explained, for it consists of schemes being hatched, of profit motivation, of intoxicated rest, of bestial pleasures. But in addition to these customers whose psychology is childish and whose refinement does not even exist, there are still others upon whom a tyrannical influence acts: rich or broadly experienced customers, unconquered bachelors without a home to flee, abstemious people decrying the game, not speaking

at all, scarcely reading the newspapers. The former are the dispassion-
ate amateurs, customers who like the café, beyond any other consideration, beyond any consideration of profit, just for itself.)

The essay is a masterful psychological analysis of the spirit of the
Parisian café and of the mentality of the customers who frequent
it. Moreover, the essay examplifies admirably the tone of much of
the work. It captures the flavor of Huysmans' writing in this work,
which certainly affords a kind of "relief" to the momentum of his
spiritual interest during this spiritual period of development.

Once again, in this work Huysmans focuses his attention upon
the manufacturing district of Paris. In "Les Gobelins," for instance, he writes:

L'on songe aux cours désertes de Versailles ou aux préaux vides de
l'Institut, quand on entre dans la manufacture nationale des Gobelins.
Les cours se suivent, bordées de graves bâtisses; les fenêtres sont closes
et les rideaux tirés; l'on ne rencontre personne et l'on n'entend rien. Au
sortir de l'avenue bruyante des Gobelins, il semble que l'on tombe dans
un quartier muet de province morte; et, forcément, ces larges et mornes
maisons vous suscitent l'image du roi Louis XIV, car la plupart d'entre
elles ont gardé l'allure solennelle et pimbêche de son temps.[12]

(One reflects upon the deserted courts of Versailles or upon the empty
courtyards of the Institute, when he enters the national manufacturer
of the Gobelins. The courtyards follow one after the other, flanked by
heavy ramshackled buildings; the windows are closed and the curtains
drawn; one meets nobody and hears nothing. Coming out of the noisy
avenue of the Gobelins, one seems to fall into the mute quarter of a
lifeless province; and, inevitably, these broad and somber houses arouse
the image of Louis XIV in you, for most of them have retained the
solemn and disagreeable bearing of his epoch.)

This paragraph evidences very well the flavor of much of the writing of the book. From its lines, too, it is apparent that in this interlude, Huysmans once more has returned to the inspiration of his
Naturalist period. It is the last time that he does so in print. Never
after *De Tout* will Huysmans return to Naturalistic themes or
Naturalistic or Decadent treatment of his subject material. Henceforth he is to be upon all occasions a purely spiritual writer.

De Tout is a difficult work to assess. Some of the essays are much finer than others. Several of the more impressionistic essays, indeed, are exquisite. However, on the whole the book lacks the general substance in depth possessed by his earlier collections of prose poems. The difficulty, most probably, is simply that Huysmans has left behind him, forever, the Naturalistic and Decadent periods which inspired his more noteworthy efforts in this genre. Now, in the full bloom of the spiritual period proper, he simply finds the very form of such an essay, or prose poem, or impressionistic piece, foreign to the momentum which truly carries him forward. A hagiographer simply does not, and cannot, indulge very profitably, too long, in such a genre. Hence *De Tout* is something of a disappointment, particularly in comparison with the works that precede it and that follow it in Huysmans' spiritual period.

IX   Esquisse biographique sur Don Bosco

Huysmans published *Esquisse biographique sur Don Bosco* at Paris in 1902.

Perhaps this second hagiographical study is the most uninspiring and weakest work which Huysmans ever wrote. First, it is too short, comprising only eighty pages. Second, it is too modern for Huysmans' taste, the life and works of the nineteenth-century Giovanni Melchior Bosco not lending itself to the kind of treatment which the author so much enjoyed with the life and works of the fourteenth-century Saint Lydwine de Schiedam. Third, the physical format, with its rather amateurish illustrations, is disappointing in the extreme. The total impression left upon the reader by the short work, then, is one of great dissatisfaction. As a matter of fact, Huysmans himself admits to a kind of shame upon publishing the book.

X   L'Oblat

Huysmans published *L'Oblat* with Stock at Paris in 1903.

The oblate of whom the title speaks is Huysmans himself, at Ligugé, from the end of 1899 to the end of September, 1901. Moreover, the oblate is not only the story of Huysmans' sojourn in the shadow of the Abbey of Saint Benoît. It is also, and more importantly, the logical continuation, and culmination, of a long autobiography, of which the several parts have been scattered in Huysmans' works from the beginning: in *Marthe, Sac au dos, A Vau-l'Eau, Les Soeurs Vatard, En Ménage, En Rade,* under the Naturalist influence; in *A Rebours* and *Là-Bas,* under the Decadent influence; in *En Route* and *La Cathédrale,* under the spiritual influence. The names of the protagonist have changed during the course of this long autobiographical novel, but essentially the hero is always Huysmans himself, and often only thinly disguised. Now, in *L'Oblat* (*The Oblate*), the hero's name, again, is Durtal. It is Durtal who undergoes the deep spiritual crisis.

At the beginning of the book Durtal has been living at Val-des-Saints for more than eighteen months. Tired of Chartres, where for a time he had settled, and harassed by desultory longings for the cloister, he goes to the Abbey of Solesmes. His motive is that of reaction:

It was, in truth, no longer the iron rule of the Cistercians, with their perpetual silence, their black fast and never-ending abstinence, bound to sleep fully dressed in a dormitory, to rise at two o'clock in the morning and to work either at some handicraft or on the land. The Benedictines were allowed to speak, and on certain days to eat meat. They could undress for the night and each had his private cell; they rose at four o'clock to devote themselves to mental rather than manual work, being far busier in libraries than in the workshop or the field.[13]

and in the same connection, again:

Self-denial and penance were the aims of the Trappists, whereas the Benedictines, properly so-called, devoted themselves to the divine service of praising God. Consequently the former, impelled thereto by St. Bernard, had intensified all that was strict and harsh in the rule; on the other hand, the latter took full advantage of its kindlier and more lenient side.[14]

The change in locality and atmosphere pleases Durtal immensely. He thrives in the new surroundings. In the novel, from this point on, are detailed long confessions of the most scrupulous sort. There are discussions on the monastic life, church art, seclusion, among other topics. Secular life is reflected through Huysmans' position, by means of Durtal, his mouthpiece, on the Dreyfus affair: He sides, of course, with the Church and against Dreyfus and Jewry. Durtal continues to evolve spiritually.

It is Dom Felletin who explains to Durtal, and thus for the reader's benefit, the meaning of the oblate's calling:

First of all, we must resign ourselves to the conviction that the oblate-hood of St. Benedict will never become widely popular; it will never appeal save to a chosen few; indeed, it requires so much of candidates that is difficult to fulfil. The sole reason for its existence is the Liturgy; the life of a monk is the praise of God; the life of an oblate will also be the praise of God, reduced, however, to as much as he can give; to be a true oblate it is not enough to perform one's duties faithfully and communicate more or less frequently; one must also have a taste for the Liturgy, a love of ritual and of the symbolical; an admiration for religious art and for beautiful services.[15]

The Benedictine life exerts a great appeal on Durtal. He rhapso-dizes over the sound of bells; over monks with muffled feet enter-ing the sanctuary like wraiths; over the swish and the image of their large black cowls; over the reciting of the Psalms; over their lugubrious accents; over their every action. It is, he finds, a good life: the one for which he has always yearned.

Thus Durtal waxes eloquent, further, in the following passage:

The air seemed almost soft and Durtal before Mass had taken a walk in his garden. The little woodland walk was carpeted with violets; and the brown, sticky buds of the chestnut-trees were ready to burst, though the boughs seemed inky-black; the fruit-trees were in blossom; cherry-trees and the peach-trees were sprinkled with snow-white and pink; after the cheerless winter and the big doses of prayer in the pre-vious week, what a relief it was to reach Spring, and Easter! [16]

Life in the monastery is, for Durtal, a poem which he relishes upon every occasion. He has never been so exalted. Such moments of esthetic joy and spiritual fulfilment succeed one another in experi-ence after experience. Huysmans, in another passage, portrays Durtal in one of his final moments at the Abbaye:

Like some dismasted vessel, Durtal drifted on a sea of depression, and would surely have sunk, had it not been for the delightful companionship of Brother Blanche. He had never known before how much he had esteemed the monks. The result was a sort of mirage. He no longer saw the faults, the absurdities, the obviously human side of the monastery; the good but commonplace middle-age receded into the shade, while the two extremities, old-age and youth, stood forth in a bright light; the old monks, those brought up according to the olden standard, both dignified and deeply pious, and young novices in all the first fervour of their vocation. Thanks to those two elements there emanated from the monastery a power which in one particular resembled the power of the Liturgy; in neither case was the power very noticeable to those under its influence any more than the current to the swimmer who swims with it; but as soon as the current ceases, as soon as the influence is removed, then one becomes painfully aware of one's loss.[17]

And Durtal is to become fully aware of this loss only as he leaves the refuge of his monastery to find again the cold crassness of the great but Godless megalopolis of Paris.

The Oblate is a great novel. Above the preoccupation with church liturgy, with medieval symbolism, with artistic independence, with monastic solitude, with all other esthetic and, indeed, even religious concerns, there rises the great self-analysis of Durtal himself. In his protagonist Huysmans has created a masterpiece of psychological study. It is in this sense, primarily, that *The Oblate* is a monument of its kind in French literature. But the book lives also through its glowing prose, always surcharged with the religious quality which it seeks to capture.

XI   Trois Primitifs

Huysmans published *Trois Primitifs* with Vanier and Messein at Paris in 1905.

Once again he composes a penetrating art study, primarily of religious art or, at least, of art on quasi-religious subjects. This, once more, is his perennial concern. In "Les Grünewald du Musée de Colmar," Huysmans writes of his topic, Grünewald:

Il est à la fois naturaliste et mystique, sauvage et civilisé, franc et retors. Il personnifie assez bien l'âme ergoteuse et farouche de l'Allemagne, agitée à cette époque par les idées de la Réforme.[18]

(At the same time he is naturalistic and mystic, savage and civilized, open and wily. He personifies rather well the quibbling and savage soul of Germany, shaken at that time by Reformation ideas.)

Huysmans is ever a perspicacious observer. He is a student not only of art, within the studies comprising the work, but also of human nature. In this respect he again records his religious anti-semitism in "Francfort-sur-le-mein" with a deft characterization of the soul of one of the Jewish centers of Europe:

Une impression de malaise très spécial vous vient dans ces casernes de luxe et dans ces rues . . . Ce que l'on éprouve, c'est surtout dans l'antipathie de ce monde des sémites qui vous entoure; ce n'est pas, en effet, une question de nationalité qui vous opprime, c'est une question de race; ce n'est pas le hessois qui vous est hostile ici, c'est le Juif. Il s'atteste partout à Francfort, et tout est assorti à son image: l'empha-tique et l'insolente opulence de cette ville, son goût de parvenue, la redondance de son éclairage et de ses boutiques, tout est en accord avec les appétances, avec la tenue, avec les instincts même du Juif.[19]

(A quite distinctive kind of discomfort comes to you in these luxurious quarters and in these streets. What one feels is especially antipathy for this Jewish world which surrounds you. It is not, indeed, a concept of nationality which oppresses you; it is a fact of face. It is not the Hessian who is offensive to you here; it is the Jew. It manifests itself every-where in Frankfurt, and everything is matched to its image: The emphatic and insolent wealth of this city, its parvenu's taste, the over-flowing of its street lamps and its shops, everything is in accord with the appetites, bearing, even the instincts of the Jew.)

Here, as throughout the work, Huysmans evidences his concern with spiritual psychology, whether in religious art or in the life that gives impetus to that art. He succeeds admirably. Although *Trois Primitifs* is not one of his greater works, it is nonetheless a book of lasting importance and of special significance for his growing depth of understanding in his spiritual period.

XII   Le Quartier Notre-Dame

Huysmans published *Le Quartier Notre-Dame* with the Li-brairie de la Collection des dix at Paris in 1905.

As a study of another section of Paris, the book is not only informative but also definitive. The prose is always good and sometimes excellent. A religious atmosphere pervades the book from beginning to end. Huysmans is clearly in his religious period.

XIII   Les Foules de Lourdes (Crowds of Lourdes)

Huysmans published *Les Foules de Lourdes* with Stock, Paris, in 1906. It was an immediate and resounding success.

He wrote the book under the following circumstances. From the publication of *L'Oblat* to that of *Les Foules de Lourdes,* the author, now permanently located in his domicile in Paris, reknotted his old friendships. He made no new acquaintanceships. He devoted himself entirely to religion, to examination of his conscience, to a few literary endeavors, such as a preface for *A Rebours* and another preface to the religious poetry of Verlaine. In short, he gave himself over to religious considerations to the virtual exclusion of all else.

The great problem of a book like *Les Foules de Lourdes,* as Huysmans envisioned it, was to combine the Naturalistic and spiritualistic elements. He set himself to resolving it. For him Lourdes was, after all, a repulsive yet divine place, a physical hell but a paradise of the soul. As a realist but a mystic, then, he tried to reconcile these two opposite factors within his study. He succeeded admirably by combining his documentary powers of observation with a kind of spiritual infusion.

Les Foules de Lourdes is very much alive. The reader cannot fail to be deeply moved by the evocation of saintliness, by the majestic prose, by the powerful imagery, by the sweeping concepts incarnate within the cadences. The subject itself, of Christian mysticism, is ennobling. The treatment is one of utter sacredness. There is a total lack of prosaicism. Thus *Les Foules de Lourdes* is also, in its way, the very apogee of Huysmans' religious period.

XIV   Trois Eglises

Huysmans published *Trois Eglises et Trois Primitifs* with Plon-Nourrit at Paris in 1908. It was a new impression for *Trois Primitifs,* which has already been mentioned. But it was the initial publication for *Trois Eglises,* contained within the volume. There are three sections within this part of the volume, respectively entitled "La Symbolique de Notre-Dame de Paris," "Saint-Germain-l'Auxerrois," and "Saint-Merry."

In "La Symbolique de Notre-Dame de Paris" Huysmans is concerned with the fundamental concept of the cathedral, as an entity in itself, and with the nature of the symbolism of its architecture. He defines the cathedral in the following terms:

La cathédrale était donc un ensemble, une synthèse; elle embrassait tout; elle était une bible, un catéchisme, une classe de morale, un cours d'histoire et elle remplaçait le texte par l'image pour les ignorants.[20]

(Thus the cathedral was a unity, a synthesis; it included everything; it was a Bible, a catechism, an ethics class, a history course; and it replaced the written text by the visual image for the unlettered.)

Huysmans develops his symbolism elaborately. The roof of the Cathedral represents love. The tiles represent the soldiers of the Church. The cornerstones of the Cathedral represent the four Evangelists, or the four cardinal virtues. The windows represent the organs of our sense-impressions, open to the Christian world. The three great doors represent the Holy Trinity. In addition, there are many other variations of the prevailing symbolism.

In "Saint-Germain-l'Auxerrois" Huysmans waxes poetic upon occasion, while at the same time he retains his religious treatment. He writes:

Les temps sont changés; si Saint-Germain a vu les pieuses affluences et les cohues irritées ou gouailleuses, s'il a même aussi connu, pendant la Convention, les hilares assemblées de légères muscadines et de pesantes commères, réunies, devant sa porte, pour applaudir aux audacieuses et aux piètres chansons d'Ange Pitou, il ne connaît plus de foule d'aucune sorte maintenant. Ses abords sont rapidement longés par des gens en rut d'affaires et quant à son intérieur il est un des plus délaissés qui soient à Paris; sa nef ne peut même, le dimanche, à la grand' messe, malgré tous les enfants des écoles qu'on y parque, se remplir.[21]

(The times have changed; if Saint-Germain has seen the pious crowds and the irritated or waggish mobs, if it has even known too, during the convention, the hilarious assemblies of frivolous women and of sluggish gossips, gathered before its door to applaud the audacious and wretched songs of Ange Pitou, it no longer knows any kind of crowd now. Its approaches are now skirted by people busily going about their business, and as to its interior it is one of the most neglected in Paris; its nave cannot even be filled on Sundays, during high mass, despite all the schoolchildren parked there.)

The essay continues in this fashion. It is a masterpiece of observation and religious analysis.

In "Saint-Merry" Huysmans first investigates the life and works of the saint in question. In this connection he observes:

Saint Médéric ou Saint Merry n'est pas un saint sur le compte duquel les renseignements abondent. Ce que l'on connaît de sa vie peut se résumer en quelques lignes. Entré à l'âge de treize ans au monastère bénédictin de Saint Martin, situé près de la ville d'Autun où il naquit, il devint abbé de ce cloître, prit la fuit pour se retirer dans un désert et y mener l'existence des ermites et fut ramené de force par l'évêque d'Autun, au milieu de ses moines. Il s'évada de nouveau avec Saint Frodulphe, l'un de ses disciples et parvint près de Paris. Là, il découvrit, dans un petit bois, une chapelle dédiée à Saint Pierre, bâtit une cellule dans son voisinage, et après y avoir demeuré pendant deux ans et neuf mois, il y mourut le 29 août de l'année 700 et fut inhumé dans ladite chapelle.[22]

(Saint Mederic, or Saint Merry, is not a saint about whom information abounds. What we know of him can be summarized in several lines. Having entered at age thirteen the Benedictine monastery of Saint Martin, located near the city of Autun, where he was born, he became the priest of this cloister, took flight from it to retire to the wilderness and lead there a hermit's life, and was forcefully brought back to his monks by the Bishop of Autum. He escaped again with Saint Frodulphe, one of his disciples, and came to the environs of Paris. There, he discovered, in a little grove, a chapel dedicated to Saint Peter, built a cell nearby, and after remaining there for two years and nine months, he died there on August 29, 700, and was buried in the aforesaid chapel.)

This jewel of an essay proceeds from this point. Huysmans lingers over the account of the life of Saint Merry and then over the

Church dedicated to him. Slowly the essay comes to an affectionate end. Just as slowly, almost as imperceptibly, Huysmans' religious period comes to its end, too, and, indeed, his career as a
writer terminates after so many years of slow and sometimes monotonous but always affectionate toil.

CHAPTER 5

Huysmans' Worldview

WHAT, then, is the permanent value of Huysmans? How is it that he still speaks vitally to so many contemporaries? Undoubtedly there are various reasons for different readers. But the principal factor in this abiding appeal lies, most probably, in the distinctive contribution of his Decadent worldview.

I *What is Decadent Literature?*

It is mandatory, at this point, to redefine Decadence.

Now, the term "Decadent literature" does not exclusively refer, by any means, to mere involutions, subtleties, niceties, conceits, and other exotic stylizations. Indeed, the very concept of Decadent literature as one of esthetic novelty and peculiarity is almost totally fallacious. It simply does not describe the extensive body of Decadent writing in general; it does not even depict with sufficient breadth the scope of Huysmans' own writing in particular. It is axiomatic that a definition which is not even descriptive can hardly be called denotative. Moreover, such a definition, based exclusively on style, grossly oversimplifies the issue. For it takes only one factor into account, esthetics, to the virtual neglect of all the other and more central issues.

Second, the term "Decadent literature" does not refer exclusively to a body of writing about psychological aberrations and assorted perversions. Such a definition, too, fails to portray the intensely wide variety of Decadent personages. In Decadent as well as in any other fiction, obviously, there are male protagonists who are not mincing homosexuals; and with just as much evidence of fact, there are female protagonists who are not lesbians or transvestites. For instance, the familiar theme of sado-masochism, while obsessive throughout the literature of the Decadent epoch, is by no means omnipresent. As a matter of fact, Des Esseintes himself, from *A Rebours*, does not have all that twisted or "glamorous" a sexual life. Incest and bestiality, while abundant in Decadent writing, are not the sole motifs or foci of interest. Hence a denotative definition of Decadence in terms of psychology or psychiatry is quite impossible. Certainly it comes much closer to approximating the reality of Decadent literature than the esthetic approach. But ultimately it too simply does not seize the essence of Decadence. It does not fail on the grounds of oversimplification, like the notion of esthetics, but it does fall far short of the mark on the grounds of superficiality. In other words, Decadence conceived in terms of psychology or psychiatry describes much of the actual terrain of Decadent literature. Yet it does not take into full view the total picture, comprising all flora and fauna, and even including the strata and the substrata of the phenomenon of Decadence.

Essentially, thoughout his fiction Huysmans remains his own hero. He writes almost exclusively about himself and his personal experiences in his Decadent worldview. So it is that he is obsessively concerned with himself, to varying degrees of success, in his tripartite literary division, i.e., the three stages of his own evolvement.

II *Naturalism*

Perhaps it is Huysmans' first period which has least satisfactorily weathered the vicissitudes of time and the vagaries of taste. This is, of course, his Naturalistic period. During these years Huysmans waxes eloquent with a youthful exuberance that sometimes degenerates into the excesses of mere juvenilia. His tendency to expansiveness becomes tedious. His indecorum in subject matter is sometimes marked. His awkwardness in diction and his inadequacy in style are frequently pronounced. Clearly, then, Huysmans does not show himself at his best, or with the best results, during the initial period of his literary Naturalism.

Despite grave difficulties, nonetheless, a denotative definition of Decadent literature, and hence an assessment of Huysmans in this light, is possible. Such a definition, to be descriptive, must be totally inclusive. It must take into account the Decadent protagonist in his cerebral, esthetic, perverted, and cosmopolitan rôles. It must describe him vis-à-vis his counterpart, the female protagonist, the *femme fatale*. It must situate him in, or in the light of, the frame of the modern Babylon of his megalopolis, which affects his temperament so greatly. It must portray him as he effetely gasps his last dying wail of woe before the imminent disaster of his personal immolation in the ultimate world cataclysm of the *Götterdämmerung*. This world is, indeed, that of the twilight of the gods, whether envisioned as Faulkner's last ding dong of doom, or Eliot's whimper, or a blinding nuclear holocaust.

In other words, a definition of "Decadent literature" must account for all these phenomena and attitudes. And while in certain respects they represent esthetic attitudes, and while in most respects they undoubtedly represent psychological attitudes, still they also represent, more comprehensively and more basically, "religious," or at the very least "philosophical," attitudes before the fact of religious and philosophical phenomena. Thus the broadest basis for understanding Decadent literature lies on the level of religion and philosophy. It is here that the Decadent soul incarnates itself. It is here that Huysmans can be best understood.

Huysmans visualizes his Naturalistic world as a vast hell of human misery, in chiaroscuro, of the darkest tones and of the grayest bleakness. In the Naturalistic novels he sketches a sort of bourgeois but still Dantesque inferno, peopled by the ghastly phantoms of pimps, prostitutes, perverts, and sundry other dregs of the lowest strata of society. His megalopolis of Paris, in this decadent vision, is not so much that of a modern Babylon, or a transfigured imperial Rome of ancient legend, resplendent with its glory of ineffable cruelty and total depravity in the grand manner of a Heliogabalus, as that of an inordinately sprawling metropolis, in the industrialism of the late nineteenth-century, of sewers, sweat, sweatshops, and despicably petty crime, vice, and sin. Such a city, of course, represents a society in a state of utterly putrescent degeneration. Yet it is not the kind of grandiose and perhaps even noble decay in which a supremely lunatic Nero can fiddle with much regal flourish, and even babble obscene verses in a stentorian voice, while a great civilization ascends, at his very feet, in the smoke and fire of universal cataclysm and final world destruction.

Such a vision of Decadence, to say the least, is not what Huysmans presents in these early novels of the Naturalist period. Yet he does portray a world in suppurating decay.

Paris is evil, as the megalopolis, because it divorces its inhabitants, its men and women, from a warm and life-giving nature. Clearly the concept of nature is identified with the notion of goodness. No less clearly Paris is the great, or satanic, force of all that is anti-natural, i.e., of all that is artificial. Artificiality, in this sense, becomes evil. Hence Paris is active, as an agent, against what is good. Hence, too, as such a malevolent agent, as such a destructive psychic force, Paris is the incarnation of all that is supremely evil and symptomatic of what is wrong in modern society.

Within this context, Paris, the megalopolis, dehumanizes its men and women. For instance, Marthe, in the novel of that name, is not a dutiful wife or a loving mother or even a benevolent woman. She is not truly feminine. Largely through the nefarious influence of the city, she is, rather, a lustful bitch, a destructive prostitute, a pitiable victim, who, in turn, becomes a relentless bird of prey. She has been ruined by the evil forces present in the great city, Paris, which act upon her and which corrupt her. So it is that Marthe herself, in time, becomes a destructive woman. To be sure, she is not representative of the glamorous *femme fatale* of later works. Nonetheless, she can, and does, destroy. Once victimized, she now begins to victimize others. And the process continues in a kind of eternal recurrence of the very pattern of evil.

Once again, in the novel entitled with their name, the Vatard sisters are the wretched victims, as well as the sometimes unwitting victimizers, of their society. Unhappy themselves, Céline and Désirée make Cyprien Tibaille and Auguste, their respective lovers, unhappy in the miserable state of their human existence. The interplay of human emotions in this entangled affair is relatively unimportant. What is important, rather, is the fact that Céline and Désirée, too, cannot fill their natural rôles as women, i.e., as wives and mothers, because the very structure of Parisian life forbids it. They are caught in a web of circumstance. They have lost their true femininity. In that sense they are anti-natural, and they inhabit a decadent world.

Huysmans' male protagonists, during this Naturalistic period, are also anti-natural, i.e., not manly. André Jayant, from *En Mén-age*, suffers from a kind of late-romantic abulia; he is a cerebral man given to introspection at the expense of acting. Jean Folantin, from *A Vau-l'Eau*, is a prototype of this Naturalistic brand of the Decadent hero. A government functionary caught in the prison of red tape and a drab existence, he, too, goes "against the grain," so to speak, by reveling in his rêveries, by reflecting upon the ugliness of the world about him, by ineffectually grappling with the women in his life. So it is that, even in the Naturalistic world, he drifts "down stream," while the uninspiring life of a singularly bourgeois Paris bears down heavily upon him and around him.

III *Decadence*

If Joris-Karl Huysmans were known solely for *A Rebours*, his niche in French letters would still be secure and still be unique. Such is the impact of the book. Indeed, when one thinks of Decadent literature, he considers, and must necessarily consider, *A Rebours*, which is the very incarnation of the Decadent message.

Des Esseintes, the hero, as has already been discussed, inhabits a mundane world of prosaic reality in Paris. He whets his jaded senses upon all the pleasures and artificialities that a sophisticated megalopolis can give him. But even that is not enough. Thus he retires to his country manor at Fontenay in his infamous pursuit of the exquisite and rare pleasures.

While there, he is not much interested in the pursuit of such crass experience as mere sexuality. On the other hand, he gives himself over, like Epicurus, the master whose writings he adores, to a determined quest of philosophical sensualism. Hence he collects fine wines and liqueurs; he atomizes perfume pictures in the air; and he dotes upon his extensive collection of exotic plants and flowers, of which one is reputedly carnivorous. These, indeed, are among his more normal pursuits, while he shrouds himself in a self-imposed mystery in the monastic life of sorts at Fontenay.

Des Esseintes is the prototype of the Decadent hero. He has an obsessive love of everything artificial. He is afflicted with abulia; i.e., he is cerebral to the point of being incapable of action. He is passive and consequently yearns for the destructive *femme fatale*, the overbearing woman like Miss Urania, so that he might deliciously be crushed in her arms. He is esthetic. He cultivates the rarest and most titillating of sensations. In this sense, as in his sexual life, he is twisted, perverted, desiring above all the anti-natural. Of course, he is a sado-masochist. He likes to inflict torture upon others, like the young street boy, his protégé, and likes to suffer pain from certain others, too, as from Miss Urania. In short, Des Esseintes is a "mental" case, for what the term might connote. More accurately phrased, he is so esthetically oriented, or, rather, disoriented, that one might call him a "pathological" hero.

As such a protagonist, he is immortal in the annals of world literature. When one wishes to stress the type, he must necessarily refer to Des Esseintes. *A Rebours* is a great *tour de force;* Des Esseintes, a masterpiece of type creation, because he is at once individual while being universally true. There was never any hero quite like Des Esseintes before the appearance of *A Rebours,* and certainly there has never been anyone equal to him since that time. Thus Des Esseintes, as a character, deserves the supreme accolade: He broke the mold of the Decadent hero in Decadent fiction.

Là-Bas is also a masterpiece of Decadent fiction during Huysmans' second literary period.

Once again, the hero, Durtal in this instance, has all the traits of the Decadent protagonist. He is interested in art, music, literature. He is an esthete by inclination, a novelist by vocation. He is afflicted with abulia; he can work less than half the time, and then only with the gravest determination. He is, for lack of another term, somewhat "perverted" or twisted, particularly through his sado-masochism. Paris exercises an enervating effect upon him; yet he cannot force himself to leave the city which destroys him. In addition, he is consumed by a singularly unhealthy interest in satanism and the occult. It preoccupies him; it obsesses him; it takes control of his personality. In the end, indeed, this satanism almost destroys him.

In the same novel Mme Hyacinthe Chantelouve is the prototype of the *femme fatale* in the grand manner. Totally unlike Huysmans' earlier heroines, except for the fact that they too are destructive, Mme Chantelouve is beautiful and cultivated. Yet she is also a victim of society, and she victimizes others within that society. She is totally immoral. She does not understand the faintest meaning of conjugal fidelity. Her liaisons are seemingly without number, and in her love affairs she prefers and cultivates men of the cloth. She, too, is absorbed in satanism, the occult, the black mass, and all the other trappings of late nineteenth-century French mysticism. As a kind of vampire, she feeds upon her lovers, and particularly upon Durtal, and sucks from them the life-blood of their energy, their vitality. In short, Mme Chantelouve is a fatal woman, a sado-masochist, divorced from nature and natural process, who simply cannot help destroying everyone with whom she comes into contact.

No reader of Huysmans can forget these two great novels of the Decadent period: *A Rebours* and *Là-Bas*. Indeed, largely because of them, Huysmans is known almost exclusively as this kind of "decadent" novelist. These novels brought him his first great notoriety, and hence literary reputation. In large part they have insured it since that time. For they capture the essence of the Decadent soul.

IV *Spiritualism*

Huysmans leaves his more saturnine moments behind him as he enters the spiritual phase of his "decadent philosophy." This is the third period, the spiritual period, of his evolvement. It shows his final stage of thought on the fundamentally religious message which he transmits through his books on the Decadent issue.

During this period, of course, Huysmans continues his interest in art through the collection of essays entitled *De Tout*. In other words, he shows himself, as always, an esthete. His interest in religion deepens with his studies in hagiography, e.g., *Sainte Lydwine de Schiedam*. His study of the Cathedral at Chartres, in *La Cathédrale*, is monumental. Clearly, then Huysmans moves more and more deeply into the essentially religious aspects of the Decadent worldview.

This metamorphosis is seen through the author's mouthpiece, Durtal. It is he who is the Decadent hero of *Là-Bas*, where he reveals himself as conceited, sado-masochistic, sensual, and esthetically disoriented. Now Durtal undergoes a religious crisis, or conversion, in *En Route*, the account of his sojourn at the Trappist monastery at Notre-Dame d'Igny. *L'Oblat* continues the evolution of Durtal's religious character.

The changes in Durtal's personality are striking. He ceases to pursue women, albeit with difficulty. He no longer suffers from abulia. His sado-masochism falls away, like a persona, as he assumes a new and religious self. His esthetic sensitivity is no longer turned to rare books, exotic pictures, fine liqueurs, and costly wines. He is now attuned to the taste of the strong black coffee, or black bread, or diluted wine, or wholesome cheese of the monastic life. He is now enamored of the cathedrals of the Middle Ages and becomes a learned student of their art and architecture. Most importantly, of course, he discards his conceit, i.e., his satanic pride or over-concern with himself. He directs his thoughts to God and to Godliness. His purpose in life is no longer the satisfaction, or satiation, of his basest instincts: it is now to do the will of God and to obey His holy laws in every respect. In short, Durtal has become a child of the Church. He has taken refuge in the Holy Faith. He has found satisfaction in the ways of God. He has found happiness by renouncing his former decadent self.

Such is the message which Huysmans has for his readers. The Decadent hero ceases to be "decadent" by stripping himself of his perverted tastes, penchants, habits, and by submitting himself to the authority of the Holy Church. Then he no longer suffers from the malady of decadence. He is attuned to the natural order of things. For in Huysmans' concept it is the Christian message which represents the health, harmony, and beauty of nature. Salvation, hence, refers to what is natural. Decadence is identified with what is eccentric, or awry from nature; salvation, with what is congruent with nature. And salvation means the renunciation of the decadent way of life, in the negative sense. Salvation, in the positive sense, is the assumption of the Christian mode of behavior, cognizant that all mortals move in God's world and should therefore act according to His holy laws.

Doubtlessly it is in Huysmans' Decadent worldview that most contemporary readers take their interest and from which they derive a lasting understanding and appreciation of the human condition.

After all, Huysmans is not one of the greatest Naturalists. *Sac au dos* lives to the present day, and *A Vau-l'Eau* maintains its niche in French literature. But Huysmans is not so great a Naturalist as Zola or the Goncourt brothers. His *Marthe* and *Les*

Soeurs Vatard are not so good as the comparable novels on the same Naturalistic themes by many of the other Naturalistic writers. *En Ménage* is quite tedious. Clearly Huysmans is not at his best as a Naturalist writer.

In many other respects, too, Huysmans fails to measure up to the qualities demanded of a great or universal author. Some of his works, like *Là-Bas,* are too strange, too strained, much too dated as a *tour de force.* They far too clearly bear the imprint of their time. Other of his works, like *La Cathédrale,* despite their interest, become quite tedious with their innumerable *longueurs* and digressions. Certain of his works, like *L'Oblat,* are too technical for the non-Catholic reader. His psychology is, from this standpoint, so much in the lineage of Saint Thomas Aquinas that it simply does not speak to most Protestant readers. Sometimes, also, there is a forced mysticism, and too frequently there is an affected satanism. Here, too, Huysmans is not at his best.

A Rebours, of course, is his masterpiece. Undoubtedly it will be read as the great work of Decadence so long as the Decadent school holds any interest whatsoever in the history of French literature. This is natural. For here Huysmans develops the entire psychology, or, better, philosophy, or better still, religion, of the Decadent movement. Aspects of this religious orientation toward life, the so-called "decadent worldview," are present throughout all his other writing, including the earlier Naturalistic works; and they are especially present and apparent in the later spiritual period. But in this one work, *A Rebours,* the Decadent worldview is revealed, described, stated, summarized, and expounded, as it has never been developed before or since.

Huysmans is much more than simply the author of a single volume, *A Rebours.* Yet it should be clear, by now, that he is the author of a single philosophy, the Decadent worldview. It is in this worldview that he captivated the mind of his generation. It is through this worldview that he survives today: And it should never be forgotten that this Decadent worldview, as Huysmans understood it, is undoubtedly and primarily a religious worldview.

Notes and References

CHAPTER ONE

1. Quoted in Robert Baldick, *The Life of J.-K. Huysmans* (Oxford, England, 1955), p. 91.

CHAPTER TWO

1. *A Dish of Spices,* translated by Samuel Putnam in *Down Stream* (Chicago, 1927), p. 192.
2. *Ibid.,* p. 194.
3. *Ibid.,* p. 221.
4. *Marthe,* translated by Samuel Putnam in *Down Stream* (Chicago, 1927), p. 38.
5. *Ibid.,* p. 96.
6. *Les Soeurs Vatard* (Paris, 1928), p. 17.
7. *Ibid.,* p. 158.
8. *Ibid.,* p. 159.
9. *Ibid.,* p. 227.
10. *Croquis parisiens* (Paris, 1928), p. 133.
11. *Ibid.,* p. 148.
12. *Ibid.,* p. 163.
13. *En Ménage* (Paris, 1928), p. 32.
14. *Ibid.,* p. 71.
15. *Ibid.,* p. 93.
16. *Ibid.,* p. 288.
17. *Ibid.,* p. 386.
18. *Down Stream,* p. 185.

CHAPTER THREE

1. *Against the Grain,* translated by John Howard (New York, 1922), p. 84.
2. *Ibid.,* p. 78.
3. *Ibid.,* p. 87.
4. *Ibid.,* pp. 127–28.
5. *Ibid.,* p. 99.

6. *Ibid.*, p. 107.
7. *Ibid.*, p. 211.
8. *Ibid.*, p. 332.
9. *Ibid.*, p. 337.
10. *Ibid.*, p. 339.
11. *En Rade* (Paris, 1928), p. 59.
12. *Ibid.*, p. 227.
13. *Ibid.*, p. 244.
14. *Un Dilemme* (Paris, 1928), p. 231.
15. *Ibid.*, p. 158.
16. "Of Dilettantism," in *Down Stream* (Chicago, 1927), p. 270.
17. "Degas," *ibid.*, p. 281.
18. *Ibid.*, p. 279.
19. "Gustave Moreau," *ibid.*, p. 272.
20. "Félicien Rops," *ibid.*, p. 315.
21. *Ibid.*, p. 286.
22. *La Bièvre* (Paris, 1928), p. 9.
23. *Là-Bas* (Paris, 1928), pp. 244–45.
24. *Down There* (New York, 1924), p. 14.
25. *Ibid.*, p. 23.
26. *Ibid.*, p. 206.
27. *Ibid.*

CHAPTER FOUR

1. *En Route,* translated by C. Kegan Paul (London, 1897), p. 5.
2. *Ibid.*, p. 22.
3. *Ibid.*, p. 31.
4. *Ibid.*, p. 249.
5. *Ibid.*, p. 312.
6. *Ibid.*, p. 313.
7. *Ibid.*
8. *La Cathédrale* (Paris, 1928), p. 334.
9. *La Bièvre et Saint-Séverin* (Paris, 1928), p. 149.
10. *Sainte Lydwine de Schiedam* (Paris, 1928), p. 186.
11. "Les Habitants du café," from *De Tout* (Paris, 1928), pp. 32–33.
12. "Les Gobelins," *ibid.*, p. 65.
13. *The Oblate,* translated by Edward Perceval (London, 1924), p. 1.
14. *Ibid.*, p. 2.
15. *Ibid.*, p. 168.
16. *Ibid.*, p. 199.
17. *Ibid.*, p. 292.

18. "Les Grünewald du Musée de Colmar," *Trois Primitifs* (Paris, 1905), p. 305.

19. "Francfort-sur-le-Mein," *ibid.*, p. 315.

20. "La Symbolique de Notre-Dame de Paris," *Trois Eglises* (Paris, 1928), p. 173.

21. "Saint-Germain-l'Auxerrois," *ibid.*, p. 220.

22. "Saint-Merry," *ibid.*, pp. 223–34.

Selected Bibliography

PRIMARY SOURCES

Le Drageoir à épices. Paris: Dentu, 1874.
Marthe, histoire d'une fille. Brussels: Gay, 1876.
Les Soeurs Vatard. Paris: Charpentier, 1879.
Sac au dos (in *Les Soirées de Médan*). Paris: Charpentier, 1880.
Croquis parisiens. Paris: Vaton, 1880.
En Ménage. Paris: Charpentier, 1881.
A Vau-L'Eau. Brussels: Kistemaeckers, 1882.
L'Art moderne. Paris: Charpentier, 1883.
A Rebours. Paris: Charpentier, 1884.
En rade. Paris: Tresse et Stock, 1887.
Un Dilemme. Paris: Tresse et Stock, 1887.
Certains. Paris: Tresse et Stock, 1889.
La Bièvre. Paris: Genonceaux, 1890.
Là-Bas. Paris: Tresse et Stock, 1891.
En Route. Paris: Tresse et Stock, 1895.
La Cathédrale. Paris: Stock, 1898.
La Bièvre et Saint-Séverin. Paris: Stock, 1898.
La Magie en Poitou; Gilles de Rais. Ligugé, 1899.
La Bièvre; Les Gobelins; Saint-Séverin. Paris: Société de Propagation des Livres d'Art, 1901.
Sainte Lydwine de Schiedam. Paris: Stock, 1901.
De Tout. Paris: Stock, 1902.
Esquisse biographique sur Don Bosco. Paris, 1902.
L'Oblat. Paris: Stock, 1903.
Trois Primitifs. Paris: Vanier and Messein, 1905.
Le Quartier Notre-Dame. Paris: Librairie de la Collection des Dix, 1905.
Les Foules de Lourdes. Paris: Stock, 1906.
Trois Églises et Trois Primitifs. Paris: Plon-Nourrit, 1908.
In collaboration with Léon Hennique:
Pierrot sceptique. Paris: Rouveyre, 1881.

Works with prefaces by Joris-Karl Huysmans

Bois, Jules. *Le Satanisme et la magie*. Paris: Chailley, 1895.

Broussolle, Abbé J.-C. *La Jeunesse du Pérugin et les origines de l'École ombrienne*. Paris: Lecène-Oudin, 1901.

Cazals, F.-A. *Paul Verlaine, ses portraits*. Paris: Bibliothèque de l'Association, 1896.

Dutilliet, Abbé Henri. *Petit Catéchisme liturgique*. Paris: Bricon, 1895.

Gourmont, Remy de. *Le Latin mystique*. Paris: Mercure de France, 1892.

Hannon, Théodore. *Rimes de joie*. Brussels: Kistemaeckers, 1881.

Verlaine, Paul. *Poésies religieuses*. Paris: Messein, 1904.

English Translations

Dish of Spices, translated by Samuel Putnam in *Down Stream*. Chicago: Covici, 1927.

Marthe, translated by Samuel Putnam in *Down Stream*. Chicago: Covici, 1927.

Sac-au-dos, translated by L. G. Meyer in *Short Story Classics*, edited by William Patten. New York: Collier, 1907.

Down Stream, translated by Samuel Putnam. Chicago: Covici, 1927.

"Of Dilettantism" (an excerpt of one essay from *L'Art moderne*), translated by Samuel Putnam. Chicago: Covici, 1927.

Against the Grain, translated by John Howard. New York: Lieber and Lewis, 1922.

"Degas," "Felicien Rops," and "Gustave Moreau" (three essays from *Certains*), translated by Samuel Putnam in *Down Stream*. Chicago: Covici, 1927.

Down There, translated by K. Wallis. New York: Boni, 1924.

En Route, translated by Kegan Paul. London: Paul, Trench, Trubner, 1896.

The Cathedral, translated by Clara Bell. London: Paul, Trench, Trubner, 1898.

St. Lydwine of Schiedam, translated by Agnes Hastings. London: Paul, 1923.

The Oblate, translated by E. Perceval. London: Paul, 1924.

Grunewald (two essays from *Trois Primitifs*), translated by Robert Baldick. London: Phaidon Press, 1958.

Crowds of Lourdes, translated by W. H. Mitchell. London: Burns, Oates, 1925.

Selected Bibliography

SECONDARY SOURCES

BACHELIN, HENRI. *J.-K. Huysmans*. Paris: Perrin, 1926. Primarily a biographical study. Emphasizes naturalistic traits and Catholic aspects.

BALDICK, ROBERT. *The Life of J.-K. Huysmans*. Oxford, England: Oxford University Press, 1955.
The most balanced study in French or English. A definitive study of the man and writer.

BILLY, ANDRÉ. *Huysmans et Cie*. Paris: Nizet, 1963.
In this study of several important French writers of the nineteenth and twentieth centuries, one essay, an admirable one, is concerned with Huysmans and his friends at Lyons. Valuable for this period of Huysmans' life and intellectual and spiritual development.

BLANDIN, HENRI. *J.-K. Huysmans*. Paris: Maison du Livre, 1912.
Three essays, one each on the man, the writer, and the Catholic apologist. Highly interpretative.

BRUNNER, H., and CONINCK, J. L. DE *En Marge d'A Rebours*. Paris: Dorbon-Aîné, 1929.
A close and often textual study of the masterpiece in all its respects.

CEVASCO, GEORGE A. *J. K. Huysmans in England and America*. Charlottesville, Virginia: The Bibliographical Society of the University of Virginia, n.d.
A brief but useful study of Huysmansiana and of the French author's literary reputation in the United Kingdom and the United States.

CHASTEL, GUY. *J.-K. Huysmans et ses amis*. Paris: Grasset, 1957.
An intensive study of his friends, mistresses, literary acquaintances, publishers, and spiritual advisors.

CRESSOT, MARCEL. *La Phrase et le vocabulaire de J.-K. Huysmans*. Paris: Droz, 1938.
The classic study of his style, diction, and word coinage.

DESCAVES, LUCIEN. *Les Dernières années de J.-K. Huysmans*. Paris: Albin Michel, 1941.
Focuses on the Catholic period and on the terminal illness.

——————. *Deux Amis: J.-K. Huysmans et l'Abbé Mugnier*. Paris: Plon, 1946.
A comprehensive study of the delicate relationship of the writer and his spiritual mentor.

HUNEKER, JAMES. *Egoists: A Book of Supermen*. New York: Scribner, 1909.

A sympathetic essay on the blatant naturalist and decadent.

LAVER, JAMES. *The First Decadent: Being the Strange Life of J. K. Huysmans*. London: Faber and Faber, n.d.

An informative, interesting, but sometimes inaccurate popularization of the man and his work.

LOBET, MARCEL. *J. K. Huysmans ou le témoin écorché*. Lyons and Paris: Vitte, 1960.

A psychological study of his religious and philosophical agony.

RIDGE, GEORGE ROSS. *The Hero in French Decadent Literature*. Athens, Georgia: The University of Georgia Press, 1961.

Analyzes the decadent aspects of Huysmans' work.

SEILLIÈRE, ERNEST. *J.-K. Huysmans*. Paris: Grasset, 1931.

An eclectic evaluation, chronologically developed, book by book, theme by theme.

Index